W9-CFQ-436

THE
LOAVES AND FISHES
PARTY COOKBOOK

ALSO BY ANNA PUMP WITH GEN LeROY

The Loaves and Fishes Cookbook

THE LOAVES AND FISHES PARTY COOKBOOK

ANNA PUMP AND SYBILLE PUMP

WITH GEN LeROY

ILLUSTRATED BY MELANIE PARKS

1817

HARPER & ROW, PUBLISHERS • NEW YORK

GRAND RAPIDS, PHILADELPHIA, ST. LOUIS, SAN FRANCISCO
LONDON, SINGAPORE, SYDNEY, TOKYO, TORONTO

THE LOAVES AND FISHES PARTY COOKBOOK. Copyright © 1990 by Anna Pump and
Sybille Pump. All rights reserved. Printed in the United States of America. No
part of this book may be used or reproduced in any manner whatsoever without
written permission except in the case of brief quotations embodied in critical
articles and reviews. For information address Harper & Row, Publishers, Inc.,
10 East 53rd Street, New York, N.Y. 10022.

FIRST EDITION

Designed by Helene Berinsky

Library of Congress Cataloging-in-Publication Data

Pump, Anna.
   The Loaves and Fishes party cookbook / Anna Pump, Sybille Pump, with
Gen LeRoy.—1st ed.
     p. cm.
   ISBN 0-06-016222-8
   1. Entertaining. 2. Cookery. 3. Menus. 4. Loaves and Fishes (Store:
Sagaponack, N.Y.) I. Pump, Sybille. II. LeRoy, Gen. III. Title.
TX731.P86   1990   89-46112
642′.4—dc20

90 91 92 93 94 DT/RRD 10 9 8 7 6 5 4 3 2 1

To all our loyal customers

ACKNOWLEDGMENTS

For their help and encouragement the authors wish to thank Alison Bond, Emma Walton, Susan Friedland, and Nicholas Noyes.

CONTENTS

- -

INTRODUCTION

It's been ten years since the day I unlocked the door of Loaves and Fishes with my own key and walked through the empty store, knowing it was the place I had always dreamed of owning. It doesn't seem possible that time has raced by so quickly. I still have such strong recollections of whitewashing the walls, setting up the food counters, cleaning the freezers and shelves. I remember cutting wildflowers from a field nearby and arranging them in a pretty pitcher I had brought with me from the Scandanavian farmhouse where I grew up—a pitcher my mother seemed always to have filled to the brim with fresh milk or thick cooled cream.

I found an old picnic table at a yard sale, shoved it into my small car, bumped along the country road, pulled into the back of Loaves and Fishes, and somehow managed to drag it around the side and set it under an old mimosa tree. It became a private dining area where Detlef, my husband, and I would steal away to have twenty-minute lunches together when business grew more hectic.

I started a small herb garden out back that grew and multiplied until it now yields the most generous quantities of fragrant herbs, which I use in all my cooking.

I have always had a strong passion for good food, and I think I have passed this along to my daughter, Sybille.

Growing up on a large working farm where my family not only harvested a wide variety of vegetables and wheat, but also raised cattle, pigs, chicken, ducks, and geese, meant that fresh produce, meats, poultry, and dairy products were always accessible. Cooking for twelve to fifty people was commonplace. I helped my mother with all the preparations—and from doing this learned almost everything there was to know about the adventurous art of cooking, its perils and its glorious rewards. Studying with master chefs later on gave me added confidence, but those formative years were the best.

Business at Loaves and Fishes increased rapidly. We went from baking 50 loaves of French bread a day to 200. The number of bran, blueberry, carrot, pumpkin, cranberry muffins, croissants, and scones quadrupled. Our pies, tarts, frittatas, and salads sold out almost as soon as they were carted from the kitchen to the front of the store. It inspired me to search for and experiment with new recipes that would surprise and delight our discerning customers.

The first request for outside catering came shortly after we opened. A customer who had orginally planned on marrying in the city had had a sudden change of heart and wanted the reception to take place at her beach house in Wainscott, L.I., a village very close to our store. Sixty guests had been invited. Her house was very small, so it was decided that a buffet should be set up on the outside deck. Sixty people on a deck? I asked Detlef, who is a master builder, to drive over with me, and while I went over the menu with the future bride, Detlef checked out the supporting beams.

Her kitchen was minute, with only an unreliable oven, a suspiciously old toaster, no counter space, an erratic refrigerator, and no pan larger than a spaghetti pot. All the cooking would have to be done at Loaves and Fishes and transported there. The reception was only a few days off, so I knew this would require extraordinary precision and planning. More than ever, I wanted everything to go as smoothly as possible for the sake of the bride and groom. It had to be a truly romantic, memorable day.

I didn't have a van, so I ended up making five trips between our kitchen and her home—bouncing over bumpy roads, my hand anchoring the food trays to the seat next to me. Into the oven they'd go, one to each rack. I covered each roasting pan with a baking sheet, improvising shelves where the French loaves could warm. Surprisingly, the wedding cake fit perfectly into my hatchback trunk, although unfortunately I had to travel at about two miles an hour with impatient farmers beeping at me from behind!

I threw crisp white linen tablecloths over practically every surface and brought over my collection of antique water pitchers and filled them with flowers. My silver candelabras gave the tiny beach house a touch of elegance.

Sybille, temporarily home from college, helped. The bartender I had hired phoned at the last minute to announce that he had the flu, so I pressed Detlef into service. Our son Harm, visiting that weekend, was immediately employed as a waiter.

Who said necessity is the mother of invention? We cleaned the unused window boxes, filled them with ice, and they became our wine coolers. A delicate umbrella stand, lined with white linen, held the long sticks of French bread. Card tables side by side and covered with a beautiful cloth became an instant bar. We moved the speakers so that the music could drift outside and blend with the sound of the crashing surf. Torches were set around, not only for illumination but also to discourage mosquitoes.

Looking back I can't recall what, if anything, went wrong. All I can remember is that it was both romantic and loads of fun and, as it turned out, a prophetic prelude to what was to come.

We began to be called upon to cater all sorts of events, from intimate dinners to princely parties, each with its own individual personality.

I bought two white vans for transporting food, spent my quiet moments trying to invent more time-saving methods, somehow developed an inner clock and a sixth sense to protect us from unexpected calamities, and all the while felt thoroughly revitalized by the challenge of creating new menus that would excite and intrigue our growing clientele. And then a wonderful thing happened. Sybille graduated college, took a degree in cooking, and joined me. It was as if the past was repeating itself. There she was, standing by my side, functioning as I had done with my own mother. It was a wonderful feeling.

Together we built the catering business step by step, and as it grew, a family feeling blossomed within our store. Many people who started with us years ago are still with us today, anticipating our needs, understanding the nature of party giving—simplifying the work. We recently catered a luncheon wedding for 200, a cocktail celebration for 125, and a dinner for 80 all in the same day. This is not unusual during our summer season, yet twenty years ago no one could have convinced me that someday I would be operating as a caterer on such a grand scale—and more amazingly, without the slightest hesitation.

Every day we answer calls from customers asking for advice about party giving or discuss it over the counter in the front of the store. There seems to be a genuine interest in home entertaining, and that, I suppose, is the main reason for wanting to do this book. To help others bring the art of dining back to the home.

What could be better than a feeling of absolute confidence when throwing a party for ten, twenty, or forty people, knowing you will be able to plan, prepare, and present the meal on your own, without tying yourself to the kitchen, and better still, treating yourself as one of the guests. It is possible.

Sybille and I chose recipes from both our files, planned a variety of party menus, distilled them so that they are easily intelligible, attached introductions to each one, including suggestions for beforehand planning, shopping, and general hints. In other words, we hope we have suggested parties that are completely manageable, flexible, and timeable so that most of the work is completed when your guests arrive. We want to help you turn ordinary events into special occasions.

Beginning in spring, the book moves through the seasons in natural sequence, indicating throughout which game, meat, fish, poultry, and produce would be the freshest and most available in those given seasons. For us, freshness is an all-important factor. Good ingredients are the basis of good cooking.

There are a few rules to remember: create an atmosphere you want, do everything as best you can, and once the party begins, if something goes wrong, carry on. Chances are no one but you will even notice. And have fun! The main point is that with each try, you will be learning and improving your own techniques. These menus were devised for the shy starter as well as the bold adventurer, but mostly for the creative cook in all of us.

We urge you to read the introductions before plunging into any of the menus, since they are designed to help you, step by step, from start to finish.

Now when Detlef and I have lunch under the mimosa tree, we aren't alone. Sybille is at our side. Her husband, Michael, who bakes all our delicious French breads and is also our bookkeeper, is there too. Stefan, their son, our wonderful, beautiful grandchild, is with us also—that is, if he isn't in the kitchen mashing something in a bowl. Sometimes, if they can break away, Harm and his wife, Nancy, drive in from New Jersey and join us on a workday, chipping in to help. Some afternoons the company at the table expands even more; farmers dropping by to deliver produce, the fabulous people who work in the front of the store serving our customers, or those who work in back at the heart of our shop, the kitchen.

Glancing around at all those familiar faces makes me realize just how cyclical life really is. After all these years—and so many miles away from the farm where I was born—here I am, sitting at a large table just like the one at home, involved in work that's both immensely challenging and infinitely fulfilling, and best of all, surrounded by the people I love.

THE
LOAVES AND FISHES
PARTY COOKBOOK

PARTY ESSENTIALS

A friend of mine who lives in an apartment and loves entertaining invested in two 6-foot collapsible serving tables. One she stores behind a sofa, the other one slides under her children's beds. Another friend of mine had a table made that folds into the wall, very much like a Murphy bed. When she's ready to entertain, she opens thin double doors and out it comes, supported by one very strong leg. She also bought six folding chairs, which when not in use are hung on hooks behind a door that always stays open.

Having enough space for a party is not generally a primary concern of people who own their own homes; in the summer, their gardens double as another room, and any table can be used as a buffet.

You must, however, have an adequate supply of tablecloths and napkins. Buy a couple of hurricane lamps with candles for outdoor entertaining. Scented torches, too, make a big difference when you're hosting a party on a summer's night. The torches have a dual function—they provide light and deter pesky mosquitoes.

Large, clean refuse bins lined with plastic can substitute as drink coolers. What we do is stand bottles on the bottom of the bin, drop in some ice, add another layer of bottles, and so on, until it's full. Sybille prefers to put the bottles in plastic bags first, securing the tops. This way the wine and champagne bottles don't get sopping wet or lose their labels. Juices and mixers don't need to be cooled since they are generally served over ice.

Most items can be rented for larger parties, but I've seen Sybille improvise time and again when plans went awry. She's used large crocks as ice containers, laundry baskets, even planters, and once a tall-sided children's wagon that could be pulled along with a handle. She's often used empty flowerpots as ice buckets, which she nestled inside pretty baskets. Baskets are very important—lined with napkins they become serving receptacles, or as I mentioned they can be a wonderful way to mask less-attractive containers.

Remember, it takes two hours for wine or champagne to chill. The amount of wine you purchase really depends on how much you want to serve. One bottle yields six 8-ounce servings. We usually figure on two to three glasses per person. Very important items not to forget, of course, are the bottle openers. Have three handy.

I own a wonderful picnic hamper. It's been in the family for years. Lined with cotton, with elastic bands to stabilize the bottles, compartments for cutlery, it's great. You can make do with various substitutes, but I think buying one is a very sound investment. Nowadays they are insulated to keep foods as fresh as possible over a long period of time. In any case, having a couple of reusable ice bags on hand for picnics and beach parties is a very good idea. They keep food and drinks cool for up to three hours.

THE PARTY SHELF

Set aside a shelf in your closet for only party supplies. This should include at least forty-eight to sixty napkins and four or five floor-length tablecloths for your buffets, bars, and dining room table. Look for water pitchers, plates, and serving trays at yard sales. You'll need at least six pitchers, forty-eight cups and saucers, forty-eight plates, and forty-eight 9-inch dessert plates, which we also find to be the best size for first courses and salads. I have a friend who wisely buys only mismatching dishes. They not only look great on the buffet table, but when one of them breaks she doesn't have to worry about whether her pattern is suddenly out of stock. Off she toodles to the next rummage sale, where she buys other plates of approximately the same

size. Another friend only keeps white plates. These too are very easily replaced.

You'll need an assortment of glasses: seventy-two drinking glasses and wineglasses. And extra sets of cutlery, which include long-handled serving spoons, forks, and ladles for larger buffets. You'll also need a thirty-five-cup electric coffee maker. It can always make less. Extra sugar bowls and creamers and extra sauce or condiment bowls should be on your list, too.

Two serving platters, 18 x 14 x 1½ inches, are a must. Ample and sturdy, they are perfect for meals ranging from twenty to forty people. You'll also need an assortment of shallow bowls, approximately 12 to 14 inches in diameter, for salads, vegetables, and soups.

Flat cake plates with 1-inch rims are compulsory. Not only can they be used for cakes, frittatas, and tarts, but they are perfect for hors d'oeuvres, cheeses, mounds of fruit, or creamy dips surrounded by vegetable spears. You'll need 14-inch, 12-inch, and 10-inch cake plates. Don't forget cake and pie cutters and servers.

Somewhere on the shelf should go a large punch bowl and ladle, and two large salad bowls, 16 inches in diameter and about 5 or 6 inches deep, also decent and manageable salad servers. Long-handled tongs are great for picking up pieces of meat, salads, pasta, asparagus spears, vegetables—almost anything.

Save your special china, fine glassware, and silver for those intimate dinners around your dining-room table. With these essential party supplies stored on your shelves, be assured that you are completely equipped to plan any party in this book—from the smallest picnic under the stars to a wedding reception for forty—and serve it with absolute confidence.

THE SOPHISTICATED KITCHEN

"A good worker is only as good as his tools," so the saying goes. A sophisticated kitchen means a wise kitchen, one with only top-quality equipment. Use only heavy-bottomed saucepans with tight-fitting lids. Aluminum with stainless steel lining that won't dent or corrode is the best. In addition to the pans you already have, you will need a 2-quart, 6-quart, and 10-quart saucepan, all with tight-fitting lids. These are great for blanching vegetables and making sauces, soups, and stock.

So far as range-to-oven cookware goes, add to your supply a 12-inch sauté pan, 2½ inches deep; a 14-inch sauté pan, 3 inches deep; and a 14-inch sauté pan, 6 inches deep. They should have straight sides, metal handles, and tight-fitting lids. The deepest sauté pan, 14 x 6 inches, should have handles on both sides for easy lifting. It's the kind of pan that is excellent for slow-browning meats on top of the stove and then, with its cover, you can pop it into the oven for perfect braising. It is good, too, for cooking any meat or poultry that requires slow cooking on top of the range. I find the largest sauté pan to be the most valuable for large gatherings. It is just right for stews or jambalaya.

You'll need two 6-inch omelet or crêpe pans, which will come in handy when preparing quick breakfasts or brunches. Make sure you have 12-inch and 16-inch skillets for cooking Chicken Burgers or Salmon Cakes, and browning meats, fish, and poultry. Light and easy to use, these pans were designed for quick sautéing over high heat when you need to maneuver the pan with one hand while stirring the food with the other.

I'm sure you have a 6-gallon pot for lobsters or corn, but I'll mention it anyway.

For roasting, I use a 16 x 12-inch roasting pan, 2½ inches deep, and an 18 x 12-inch pan, 3½ inches deep—great for large birds such as turkey and goose. Pans this size are also terrific for reheating ragoûts, stews, and left-overs in the oven.

Chief on your list should be a 17 x 10 x 2½-inch oval casserole, and two 13 x 9 x 2-inch oval casseroles. Invest in ones that can go from oven to table. It will be money well spent, since they last almost forever and can double as serving dishes.

For draining large amounts of pasta or vegetables, you'll need a 14-inch colander. Also two wire-mesh, long-handled skimmers that cooks call "spiders," and a long-handled, 1-cup soup ladle.

I'm sure you have a variety of stainless steel and ceramic mixing bowls. Lightweight ones are good for gentle stirring and blending, but it's advisable to have a few heavy bowls for more vigorous stirring and whisking.

Of paramount importance are your appliances. You'll need a good-quality, heavy-duty mixer. I swear by my KitchenAid, which cuts my work in half, as does my food processor. Make sure you have a julienne attachment as it will save you tons of time. You'll need a good blender, too, one that can handle tough jobs.

For baking, I use only heavy-duty aluminum pans. You should have at least 2 baking sheets, each 17 x 12 x 1 inches. Thin pans bend in the oven, bake unevenly, and ruin your food. You'll need one 6-inch, one 8-inch, two 9- or 9½-inch, one 10-inch, and one 12-inch springform pan. Cakes can be removed quite easily from this type of pan—you can slide them onto the serving platter quickly, without damaging their shape.

If you don't own a Bundt pan, buy one, as well as a loose-bottomed, 10-inch tube pan. Also necessary for making breads are at least two 9 x 5 x 3-inch loaf pans.

For tarts you'll need two 9-inch loose-bottom pans, and one 12-inch tart pan. Be sure to have a couple of muffin tins and madeleine tins, too.

Corning Ware has attractive and inexpensive plain glass bowls that go from freezer to oven to table. I suggest you buy a set of 6-quart, 8-quart, 10-quart, and 12-quart bowls. You'll keep finding more and more uses for them: hot or cold soufflés, purées, potato gratin, as serving bowls, salad bowls—the possibilities are endless.

When I was teaching cooking classes I tried to stress the importance of owning top-quality knives. Bread should be cut only with a serrated knife. A carving knife will dull if used for bread. Knives should have good balance, good handles, excellent blades, and be stored in a knife block. To sharpen them, you will need a sharpening steel. Don't put your knives in the dishwasher—just rinse them, wipe them off, and keep them sharp. You'll also need a cleaver for chopping meats and poultry. Treat it as well as you do your knives and it will last for a long, long time. Use cutting boards, reserving one for meats, another for vegetables, another for breads.

Tongs are amazingly useful in the kitchen for turning meat in a skillet or transferring almost any kind of food from pan to platter. Buy cheesecloth for fine straining, and some white cotton string for tying stuffed meats. Of course you need a rolling pin, a kitchen scale, some parchment paper, and some wire whisks. One whisk should have a large balloon for attaining maximum volume when beating eggs. Some glass jars with screw-top lids are handy for mixing salad dressings. Washable and reusable, they can also substitute for storing leftovers in the refrigerator.

Included among your basic essentials are peelers, measuring spoons and cups, timers, a salad spinner, wooden spoons, slotted spoons, rubber spatulas, and graters. I buy my natural bristle pastry and basting brushes at the hardware store. A small paintbrush of good quality is great for spreading egg wash over pie crusts, a larger paintbrush with a longer handle is marvelous for basting meats.

And finally, the most important tools in the kitchen—our hands. One of the first lessons I taught my students was how to separate eggs by breaking them open, then passing them from palm to palm, letting the whites slip through my fingers into a bowl, and ending up with perfect, unbroken yolks. Our hands are an engineering miracle, sensitive to temperature and texture, gentle, yet strong. We can go from tossing a salad without disturbing the fragility of the more delicate vegetables to kneading and punching down dough to make it a bubble-free, perfect loaf of bread. We can fold, blend, stir, and toss. Perfect tools, that you can never misplace or lose.

Look this list over carefully. Make sure everything is where it should be and within reach before starting to cook. Quality equipment, careful planning, reliable appliances, organization, and efficiency can help turn a decent cook into a master chef.

AN ESSENTIAL PANTRY

After understanding the importance of stocking the kitchen with high-quality tools, equipment, and appliances, the cook should next look to the pantry. A well-stocked pantry is as important to a cook as the food he or she plans to prepare. Here are some pantry essentials, as well as information on how they should be stored and how long they last.

Hazelnuts, almonds, pecans, walnuts, and sesame seeds can be kept any length of time if stored in a freezer. Bread crumbs, too. Yellow cornmeal, unbleached flour, and whole wheat flour will last from six to eight weeks in a dry place, but if you want to keep them longer, they should be stored in a freezer where they will last for as much as a year.

There are recipes in this book that call for dried apricots. They, along with prunes and shredded coconut, can be stored in the freezer if infrequently used because their shelf life is only three months. I also recommend stocking cans of Italian plum tomatoes, crushed tomatoes, tomato paste, and flat anchovies. They won't spoil and will eventually come in handy for sauces and dressings.

You should have baking powder, baking soda, Belgian chocolate, chocolate chips, and cocoa powder. These will last a long time if stored in a dry place at room temperature. Include salt, cornstarch, oatmeal, Basmati and Arborio rice, granulated sugar, confectioners' sugar, and light and dark brown sugar. Purchase active dry yeast from your health-food store and store it in your refrigerator.

I buy only imported olive oil from Tuscany—first press, extra-virgin olive oil, which has a distinct, rich, fruity taste that allows for a little to go a long way. A light olive oil is good for cooking, although peanut oil is best for frying. It has a higher threshold for heat and doesn't burn. I use safflower oil in baking and toasted sesame oil in a lot of recipes. Stock up on red, white, and sherry vinegars, and a really good Balsamic vinegar, which has a rich, woodsy taste. You should also have red pepper flakes, black peppercorns, capers, soy sauce, Tabasco, Dijon mustard, and mango chutney.

For enriching sauces, have a bottle of French brandy on hand, some Grand Marnier, cognac, Framboise, Calvados, kahlua, Madeira, port wine, dry white wine, red wine, and sherry.

Most of the recipes in this book call for fresh herbs and spices (when they are available). To store fresh herbs, sprinkle a layer of kosher salt inside a screw-top jar, add a layer of fresh unwashed herbs, cover that with another layer of salt, add a second layer of herbs, then salt, and continue this way until the jar is filled. Herbs saved this way will last anywhere from six to eight months. All you need to do is open the jar, take out the amount you want to use, shake off the salt, rinse the herbs, dry them well, and use them. This method applies to rosemary, basil leaves, thyme, oregano and tarragon. Store-bought dried herbs will last six months on your shelves. They should be discarded after that and restocked. This includes bay leaves, thyme, tarragon, dill weed, rosemary, fennel, cayenne, caraway seeds, ground white pepper, oregano, basil, sage, coriander, turmeric, and saffron.

Curry powder should be a blend of many spices: coriander, turmeric, fenugreek, cumin, cayenne, ginger, allspice, and nutmeg. It should be the best you can find, as should be the cinnamon you buy and the allspice, cardamom, cumin seeds, cloves, and black peppercorns you use for grinding.

You should have almond extract and vanilla extract on the shelf, too. Many of the following recipes call for vanilla essence, vanilla seeds, or vanilla extract. Make your own essence and extract by placing 12 long vanilla beans in a screw-top jar. Cover them with vodka, about 3 cups, and let sit at room temperature for about three weeks. Eventually the liquid will darken, signaling that it's become extract, and the beans will soften and swell. Whenever you need vanilla essence, take out a bean, snip off the tip and squeeze the amount called for into the batter or cream. Return the bean to the bottle and it will continue to work. The extract and beans will last almost indefinitely.

No kitchen is complete without some frozen chicken, beef, and fish stock. In this book we call only for chicken stock, and here is the recipe we use.

Chicken Stock

5 pounds chicken parts (backs, necks, and wings)
Water
2 large onions, peeled and quartered
2 cloves garlic, peeled and crushed
1 carrot, trimmed
8 sprigs Italian parsley
2 bay leaves
5 sprigs fresh thyme, or 1 teaspoon dried
2 teaspoons coarse salt
1 teaspoon black peppercorns, bruised

Place the chicken in a 10-quart stockpot. Fill three-quarters full with water. Place all the ingredients in the pot, and bring to a boil. Reduce the heat, skim foam from the top, and simmer, covered, for 2 hours. Uncover, and simmer 1½ hours more.

Line a large colander with a cotton kitchen towel.

Strain the stock through the lined colander into a bowl. Discard the solids. Ladle the stock into 1-quart containers. Chill overnight. The next day, remove and discard the fat from the top of the containers. Freeze whatever you will not use within the next four days.

YIELD: APPROXIMATELY 5 QUARTS.

The following recipe is for those who prefer to make their own crème fraîche.

Crème Fraîche

Heat the heavy cream until very hot, not boiling. Pour it into a container. Stir in the buttermilk. Cover, and let stand at room temperature until very thick, about 24 hours. Store in the refrigerator for up to 3 weeks.

3 cups heavy cream

3 tablespoons buttermilk

YIELD: 3 CUPS.

Now you're ready, with everything you need to arrange, plan, and produce a party all on your own. Good luck—and bon appetit!

THE GLORIES OF SPRING

EASTER DINNER FOR EIGHT

SPRING DINNER FOR TWELVE

CHILDREN'S BIRTHDAY PARTY FOR TWELVE

INFORMAL BUFFET DINNER FOR TWENTY

ANNIVERSARY BRUNCH FOR SIXTEEN

MOTHER'S DAY DINNER FOR EIGHT

FATHER'S DAY DINNER FOR EIGHT

Spring is the most anticipated season of the year. I get an enormous rush whenever I spot young green sprouts valiantly pushing their heads up through the frosty garden, or see farmers in the wee hours of the morning making corduroy rows in the land all around us. It's the season when blustery winds give way to gentler skies, when the land takes on a lovely new mantle of green. A very short but active season that yields the tenderest asparagus, crisp spring greens, mouth-watering rhubarb, baby carrots, zucchini, miniature squash, and field berries in abundance. Lamb and spring chicken are at their finest. Herb gardens begin to emit their potent fragrances that always inspire new dishes.

Even though the season is far too brief, we have compiled a collection of interesting menus that take full advantage of the very best that spring has to offer—easy menus, both fun and challenging. Menus that begin the season indoors with a tasty and gratifying veal ragoût, stewed to perfection, and end the season with barbecued spareribs for a Father's Day Party.

There are menus for a Mother's Day meal simple enough for a child to make. And a Children's Birthday Party that includes one of Loaves and Fishes' most popular recipes—Ginger Chicken Drumsticks. There's an Easter Dinner that begins with a spicy Red Pepper Soup and Garlic Croutons, followed by delicious lamb chops napped with a delicate Mint Hollandaise, roasted young asparagus, a fabulous Rösti, and finally, a tangy Lemon Mousse and Chocolate Madeleines.

Also included is a Southern dish, inspired by our most recent trip to New Orleans—a terrific Jambalaya.

This is the time of year when I drag out my collection of china and crockery water pitchers, and stuff them with budding forsythia branches that fill the room with their sunny blossoms, or I make an arrangement of tulips, anemones, and daffodils. It's the time of year when days lengthen and the weather mellows, when doors and windows begin to stay open, when we are happily reacquainted with the casual delights of entertaining guests under brilliant blue skies or star-filled nights.

EASTER DINNER
FOR EIGHT

RED PEPPER SOUP WITH
GARLIC CROUTONS

BROILED LAMB CHOPS WITH
MINT HOLLANDAISE

ASPARAGUS ROASTED IN
OLIVE OIL

RÖSTI

LEMON MOUSSE

CHOCOLATE MADELEINES

Spring lamb, tender young asparagus, a hearty potato pancake called *rösti*, and you're all set for a wonderful Easter Dinner.

The Red Pepper Soup can be made up to 2 days ahead and stored in the refrigerator. All you need to do is pour it into a heavy saucepan and warm it over medium-high heat.

The Lemon Mousse and Chocolate Madeleines can be prepared 1 day ahead. Cover the mousse with plastic and store in the refrigerator. It can be garnished an hour before serving. The madeleines can be placed in plastic bags, kept at room temperature, and dusted with confectioners' sugar just before you transfer them to a serving plate.

Peel the asparagus the morning of your party, cover with a damp kitchen towel, and store in the refrigerator until ready to bake, which should be done just before serving.

You can marinate the lamb chops for 6 hours in the refrigerator prior to broiling, and only 30 minutes at room temperature if you intend to rustle up the meal at the last moment. They only need minutes under the broiler, and should be watched so that they don't get overdone.

The Garlic Croutons can be prepared and covered with plastic wrap a couple of hours beforehand, and when it's time to reheat the soup they can be popped into the oven to bake.

The Rösti can be made 30 minutes ahead of the meal, and kept warm in a 250-degree oven.

This meal was created for Easter, but it is so easy to prepare, it can be served even for an informal family meal.

Red Pepper Soup with Garlic Croutons

A rich, savory soup with a surprisingly light taste. It is also excellent served cold, with a dollop of sour cream.

Heat the olive oil in a heavy saucepan, add the onions, and sauté for 5 minutes. Stir in the garlic, bell peppers, potato, chili peppers, salt, and chicken stock. Bring to a boil, reduce the heat, and simmer, covered, for 30 minutes.

Remove from the heat, add the heavy cream, and let cool to room temperature.

To make the Garlic Croutons, preheat the oven to 375 degrees.

Using the flat part of a chef's knife, mash the garlic and the salt into a paste. Place in a small bowl with the olive oil and mix well.

Arrange the bread slices in a single layer on a baking sheet, and brush each top with some of the garlic-and-olive oil mixture.

Bake 10 to 12 minutes, or until crisp and golden around the edges.

To serve the soup, purée it in batches in a blender. Pour into a heavy saucepan and heat through, but do not boil. Serve in bowls, garnished with parsley. Pass the croutons separately.

YIELD: 8 SERVINGS, 2 CROUTONS PER SERVING.

¼ cup olive oil
1½ cups chopped onions
3 teaspoons minced garlic
5 cups (4 medium) seeded and chopped
   red bell peppers
1 cup peeled and coarsely chopped
   potato
2 medium dried ancho chili peppers,
   seeded
1 teaspoon coarse salt
8 cups chicken stock (page 8)
½ cup heavy cream

Garlic Croutons

2 teaspoons minced garlic
2 teaspoons coarse salt
½ cup extra-virgin olive oil
Sixteen ½-inch slices of French bread

2 tablespoons finely chopped parsley

Broiled Lamb Chops with Mint Hollandaise

This easy-to-make hollandaise also goes beautifully with Chicken Burgers. Substitute equal amounts of tarragon or oregano for the mint leaves.

MARINADE

½ cup olive oil
3 tablespoons Balsamic vinegar
2 tablespoons fresh thyme
1 tablespoon minced garlic
1½ teaspoons freshly ground black pepper
Sixteen 1¼-inch-thick loin lamb chops

MINT HOLLANDAISE

⅓ cup fresh mint leaves, loosely packed
¼ cup lemon juice
4 egg yolks
½ teaspoon freshly ground black pepper
½ teaspoon coarse salt
½ pound (2 sticks) butter, melted

Combine the marinade ingredients in a large glass or earthenware casserole. Add the chops, turning them once. Marinate for 30 minutes at room temperature, or up to 6 hours in the refrigerator.

Preheat the broiler.

Broil the lamb chops 3 inches from the heat source for 3 minutes on each side. Transfer to a large, heated serving plate.

Make the Mint Hollandaise while the chops are broiling. Place the mint leaves and lemon juice in a blender, and blend at high speed for 3 seconds. Turn the blender off, add the egg yolks, pepper, and salt, and blend for an additional second. With the blender running, add the butter in a slow stream. Blend for 2 more seconds. Pour the Mint Hollandaise into a sauceboat, and serve separately with the lamb chops.

YIELD: 8 SERVINGS.

Asparagus Roasted in Olive Oil

Preheat the oven to 450 degrees.

Brush 2 large baking sheets with some of the olive oil. Place the asparagus in a single layer in each pan. Brush the spears with the remaining olive oil, sprinkle with salt, and bake, uncovered, for 14 minutes. Transfer to a large platter, and serve hot.

3½ pounds (48 medium) asparagus, peeled
⅓ cup olive oil
1 tablespoon coarse salt

YIELD: 8 SERVINGS.

Rösti

A crusty brown top, soft buttery potatoes inside, the thyme gives it flavor, the carrots a touch of sweetness.

Pat the potatoes and carrots with paper towels until dry, and place in a large bowl. Add the salt, pepper, and thyme. Toss to blend.

Heat 8 tablespoons of butter in a large skillet. When the foam subsides, add the potatoes and carrots. Dot with the remaining butter. Cook, covered, over a medium flame for 10 to 12 minutes, or until the vegetables are tender. Remove from the heat, and invert the skillet onto a large serving plate.

5 pounds (6 to 7 large) baking potatoes, peeled and cut into ¼ x 2-inch sticks
1 pound carrots, peeled and cut into ¼ x 2-inch sticks
2 teaspoons coarse salt
1 teaspoon ground white pepper
2 teaspoons fresh thyme leaves, or ½ teaspoon dried
12 tablespoons (1½ sticks) butter

YIELD: 8 SERVINGS.

Lemon Mousse

This wonderful dessert must be chilled for at least 6 hours before serving.

1¼ cups sugar

1½ tablespoons gelatin

4 eggs, separated

¼ cup water

1⅓ cups lemon juice

2 tablespoons plus 1 teaspoon grated
    lemon peel

2 tablespoons Grand Marnier

2¾ cups heavy cream

2 tablespoons confectioners' sugar

Combine the sugar, gelatin, egg yolks, and water in a heavy saucepan. Beat with a wire whisk until creamy. Add the lemon juice, and cook over a very low heat, stirring constantly, until the mixture starts to thicken slightly. Transfer to a bowl, and chill in the refrigerator until the mixture has the consistency of unbeaten egg whites.

Stir in 2 tablespoons of the lemon peel, and the Grand Marnier. Using an electric mixer, beat the egg whites until soft peaks hold. Spoon the egg whites on top of the lemon mixture.

Using the same bowl, beat 2 cups of the heavy cream until soft peaks hold. With a rubber spatula, fold together the whipped cream, egg whites, and lemon mixture until thoroughly combined. Pour the mousse into a 3½-quart serving bowl, smooth the top, and refrigerate for 6 hours or overnight.

One hour before serving, beat the remaining heavy cream with the confectioners' sugar until soft peaks hold. Spoon into a pastry bag fitted with a star tip. Pipe the whipped cream over the lemon mousse in a criss-cross pattern. Sprinkle with the remaining lemon peel, and refrigerate until serving time.

YIELD: 8 TO 10 SERVINGS.

Chocolate Madeleines

A wicked variation on a feather-light French favorite.

Preheat the oven to 375 degrees. Butter and dust 20 aluminum madeleine molds with flour.

Melt the butter in a small saucepan and set aside to cool.

Combine the eggs, sugar, and vanilla in the bowl of an electric mixer fitted with the whisk attachment. Beat until triple in volume.

Sift together the flour, cocoa, and baking powder. Fold into the egg batter. Gently fold in the butter.

Spoon the batter into the prepared madeleine molds, filling each mold three-quarters full.

Bake 12 to 15 minutes. The madeleines are done when they spring back when lightly touched. Remove from the oven and cool 3 minutes.

Using a flexible knife, loosen the edges of each madeleine. Turn each cookie round-side-up onto a flat plate. Let cool completely. Wrap with plastic wrap and store at room temperature.

One hour before serving, dust the madeleines with the confectioners' sugar, and arrange on a serving platter.

12 tablespoons (1½ sticks) butter
3 eggs
½ cup granulated sugar
½ teaspoon vanilla extract
5 tablespoons unbleached white flour
5 tablespoons cocoa
½ teaspoon baking powder
¼ cup confectioners' sugar

YIELD: 20 MADELEINES.

SPRING DINNER
FOR TWELVE

PARMESAN PUFFS WITH
SMOKED SALMON FILLING

VEAL RAGOÛT WITH
SPRING VEGETABLES

CREAMY RISO

LIME AND CARAMEL TART

This menu was designed for early spring when the weather is still edged with a winter chill, and April showers seem to hang around a little too long. We invite our friends to sit down to a hearty Veal Ragoût, served with a Creamy Riso and the finest baby vegetables available.

We begin the evening with Parmesan Puffs, which can be made the day ahead and stored in plastic bags. I also make the salmon filling then and store that in a covered container in the refrigerator. Just before my friends arrive, I place the puffs on a baking sheet and pop them into a preheated 425-degree oven for 8 minutes to crisp, then I fill them.

Since veal is especially difficult to trim, ask your butcher to prepare it for you. The ragoût can be made 2 days ahead. Store it in the refrigerator and just before serving, reheat it in a heavy saucepan over medium heat.

When making either Riso or risotto, use Arborio rice—an Italian short-grained white rice. Add the liquid little by little, stirring constantly to keep the rice from sticking and browning. It's the stirring that creates the desired balance between the firm and chewy rice and its smooth, creamy coating. You should begin the Riso no more than 45 minutes before serving. Once it's cooked, turn off the heat and cover the pan until the rice is ready to be served.

The Lime and Caramel Tart can be made the day before and refrigerated. Sprinkle the tart with caramelized almonds just before serving.

This is an invigorating meal that warms the soul as any winter meal can do, yet employs all the benefits that spring has to offer.

Parmesan Puffs with Smoked Salmon Filling

These are excellent hors d'oeuvres that can be made with great ease and enjoyed any time of the year.

Preheat the oven to 400 degrees. Butter 2 baking sheets.

Combine the butter, cold water, and salt in a medium-size saucepan and bring to a boil. Reduce the heat, add the flour and stir quickly with a wooden spoon for about 4 to 5 minutes, until the dough becomes smooth and silky and no longer sticks to the spoon or the sides of the pan.

Transfer the dough to the bowl of an electric mixer. Add the eggs 2 at a time, beating well after each addition.

Drop 1 heaping teaspoon of batter at a time, 1 inch apart, onto the prepared baking sheets until all the batter has been used. Sprinkle with the Parmesan.

Bake 20 minutes, or until golden brown. Remove from the oven, and cool to room temperature.

Place all the filling ingredients in a medium-size bowl and mix well to blend.

Slice the puffs in half. Place 1 teaspoon of filling on 1 half of each puff, and cover with the other half. Serve with cocktails before dinner.

YIELD: 30 PUFFS.

6 tablespoons butter
1½ cups cold water
¾ teaspoon coarse salt
1½ cups unbleached white flour
6 eggs, at room temperature
½ cup grated Parmesan cheese

FILLING

½ pound smoked salmon, finely
   chopped
½ cup finely chopped scallions
1¼ cups finely chopped celery
½ cup crème fraîche (page 9)
½ teaspoon coarse salt
¾ teaspoon freshly ground black
   pepper
1 tablespoon capers, drained

Veal Ragoût with Spring Vegetables

¼ pound (1 stick) butter

8 cups finely chopped onions

7 pounds trimmed stewing veal, cut into 1½-inch cubes

¾ cups unbleached white flour

4½ cups chicken stock (page 8)

1 tablespoon coarse salt

2 teaspoons freshly ground black pepper

5 sprigs fresh thyme

36 baby carrots, scraped and left whole

1½ pounds small mushroom caps

2 pounds baby squash (green and yellow), left whole

1½ pounds fresh spinach leaves

¼ cup lemon juice

½ cup finely chopped fresh parsley

Melt the butter in a 14-inch sauté pan, 6 inches deep. Add the onions, and sauté for 15 minutes without browning. Add the veal and sauté for 15 minutes more. Sprinkle the flour over the meat. Stir to blend.

Preheat the oven to 350 degrees.

Add the chicken stock, salt, pepper, thyme, and carrots to the meat. Bring to a boil.

Transfer the casserole to the oven, and bake 1¼ hours, covered.

Add the mushrooms caps and the squash, and stir gently. Cover, and bake 20 minutes more.

Remove from the oven. Fold in the spinach and lemon juice. Serve in the casserole, sprinkled with parsley, or transfer to your favorite tureen or large crockery bowl.

YIELD: 12 SERVINGS.

Creamy Riso

This is an exceptional dish to serve with almost any savory poultry, meat, or fish dish.

3 cups Arborio rice

1 tablespoon minced garlic

1½ teaspoons coarse salt

1 teaspoon freshly ground white pepper

8 cups chicken stock (page 8)

2 tablespoons rice vinegar

Place the rice, garlic, salt, and pepper in a large heavy saucepan. Add 4 cups of the chicken stock. Bring to a boil, stirring constantly over medium heat until all the chicken stock is absorbed, about 5 minutes. Add the remaining 4 cups stock and, still stirring, return to a boil. Reduce the heat and simmer, covered, for 12 minutes. Stir in the rice vinegar, adjust the seasoning, and serve in a separate bowl with the ragoût.

YIELD: 12 SERVINGS.

Lime and Caramel Tart

*With a buttery almond crust filled with lime custard and topped
with caramelized almonds, this tart needs 6 hours to set.*

Preheat the oven to 375 degrees.

Place the flour, almonds, and brown sugar in the bowl of
a food processor fitted with a steel blade. Pulse 5 times to
blend. Add the butter, and pulse 5 times. Add the egg yolk
and cold water. Pulse 3 times. Transfer the dough to a lightly
floured countertop, and gather together into a ball.

Press the dough into the bottom and up the sides of a 12-
inch, loose-bottomed tart pan. Line with foil and fill with dry
beans. Bake for 15 minutes, remove the beans and foil, and
bake an additional 15 minutes, or until the pastry is golden.

Remove from the oven, and let cool to room temperature
before filling.

To make the filling, pour the heavy cream into a saucepan,
and bring to a boil.

Whisk together the egg yolks, vanilla, and sugar for about
2 minutes, until light. Add 1 cup of hot cream, stirring constantly. Transfer the tempered egg/cream mixture to the
saucepan with the remaining hot cream, stirring constantly.
Place over medium heat, and continue to stir until the mixture begins to thicken into a custard. Do not allow it to boil
or the eggs will curdle. Remove from the heat, and stir in the
lime peel. Pour the custard into the baked pastry shell.

Refrigerate for at least 6 hours, or overnight, until the
custard sets.

To make the topping, spread a sheet of parchment or wax
paper onto a countertop. Combine the almonds, sugar, and
lime juice in a sauté pan, and over medium heat, melt the
sugar until it begins to caramelize. Once it has turned
golden, pour the mixture onto the parchment paper. Allow
to cool for 20 minutes, or until room temperature.

Just before serving, break up the caramelized almonds and
sprinkle over the custard. Transfer the tart from the pan to a
large flat cake plate. Cut into 12 wedges and serve.

YIELD: 12 SERVINGS.

PASTRY

1½ cups unbleached white flour
1 cup sliced almonds, skin intact
¼ cup light brown sugar
12 tablespoons (1½ sticks) cold butter,
    cut into 12 pieces
1 egg yolk
3 tablespoons cold water

LIME CUSTARD FILLING

4 cups heavy cream
8 egg yolks
2 teaspoons vanilla extract
½ cup granulated sugar
1 tablespoon grated lime peel

TOPPING

1 cup sliced almonds, skin intact
½ cup granulated sugar
1 tablespoon lime juice

CHILDREN'S BIRTHDAY PARTY
FOR TWELVE (AGES 5 TO 12)

LEMONADE WITH MINTED
ICE CUBES

LOAVES AND FISHES
GINGER DRUMSTICKS

OVEN-ROASTED ZUCCHINI
ROUNDS

DILL PASTA

BANANA BIRTHDAY CAKE

Sybille created this party menu for a friend whose daughter Rachel was celebrating her seventh birthday. Rachel, who wanted to help with the preparations, came along to the meeting to offer her input.

Ginger Drumsticks are a big favorite at Loaves and Fishes. Many of our customers asked that we include the recipe in this book. They're a particular favorite of Rachel's, too; she told Sybille that they'd be great for a party because of their built-in handles. The drumsticks can be prepared 2 days before the party, covered, and refrigerated. All you need to do is put them in a preheated 350-degree oven for about 20 minutes to warm them.

Dill Pasta made with curly fusilli is a very popular dish that we make several times a day to keep at the ready for our takeout customers. It's simple to prepare, very tasty, and can be made the day before the party. Cover and refrigerate the pasta salad, and serve it either chilled or at room temperature.

Roasted slices of crisp zucchini round out the meal very nicely. They are simple to prepare and assemble shortly before the party begins. We find it to be one of the most satisfying and easy ways to present vegetables. Crisped on the outside, yet maintaining the fresh, vegetably taste inside.

Make and frost the birthday cake the night before, and store in the refrigerator. Remove it an hour before the party. You will best appreciate the full potency of the banana flavor when the cake is served at room temperature. The lemonade should also be made the night before so it can chill overnight.

This party was an enormous success, and long after it was over we had parents dropping in or phoning us for recipes. They all shared one common feeling—they were happy that the party introduced nutritiously sound food that their children enjoyed. We felt we had to include this menu because of its simplicity and delectability.

Lemonade with Minted Ice Cubes

Finding mint leaves frozen in their ice cubes is a great conversation topic for six-year-olds. This, of course, must be prepared in sufficient time for the cubes to freeze. Minted ice cubes are also wonderful in iced tea.

Fill 3 icecube trays with water. Drop a mint leaf into each compartment, and freeze overnight.

Place the lemons, sugar, and cold water in a stainless steel or enameled pot. Bring the liquid to a boil, and stir until the sugar melts, about 5 minutes. Remove from the heat, cool, and refrigerate until chilled.

Add the lemon juice. Fill a glass or ceramic pitcher half full of minted ice cubes. Pour the lemonade into the pitcher, and garnish with the mint sprigs.

36 mint leaves, washed
2 lemons, cut into 8 sections each
3 cups sugar
12 cups cold water
4 cups freshly squeezed lemon juice
4 sprigs fresh mint

YIELD: 16 SERVINGS.

Loaves and Fishes Ginger Drumsticks

6 pounds (30 medium) chicken
   drumsticks
½ cup peeled and coarsely chopped
   fresh gingerroot
¼ cup minced garlic
I cup coarsely chopped onions
¾ cup soy sauce
I cup honey

Preheat the oven to 350 degrees.

Arrange the drumsticks in a 16 x 12 x 3-inch roasting pan. Place the ginger, garlic, onions and ¼ cup of the soy sauce in the bowl of a food processor fitted with a steel blade. Process 15 seconds, and scrape down the sides of the bowl. Process 10 seconds more. Add the remaining soy sauce and the honey, and process another 10 seconds. Pour the sauce over the chicken. Cover with aluminum foil, and bake for 2 hours. Remove and discard the foil, and bake for an additional 45 minutes.

Serve on individual plates, with the zucchini and pasta.

YIELD: 30 DRUMSTICKS, 12 SERVINGS.

Oven-Roasted Zucchini Rounds

4 pounds zucchini, sliced into
   ¼-inch-thick rounds
½ cup olive oil
I teaspoon salt
½ teaspoon freshly ground black
   pepper

Preheat the oven to 375 degrees.

Brush a 14 x 10 x 2-inch casserole lightly with olive oil. Arrange the zucchini slices in one layer of slightly overlapping rows. Brush the tops with olive oil. Sprinkle with salt and pepper.

Bake 25 minutes. Serve hot.

YIELD: 12 SERVINGS.

Dill Pasta

We recommend fusilli for this salad because the ingredients cling to this pasta better than they do any other, making a versatile dish that goes well with poultry, fish, or meat and can be served chilled or at room temperature any time of the year.

Drop the pasta into 8 quarts of boiling water. Cook for 11 to 13 minutes, stirring now and then, until the pasta is al dente. Drain in a colander, and transfer to a large serving bowl.

Add the remaining ingredients, and toss to blend well. Serve on the same plate with the chicken and zucchini.

YIELD: 12 TO 14 SERVINGS.

6 cups (1½ pounds) fusilli
1 cup finely chopped red onions
2 cups finely chopped dill pickles
1 cup finely chopped red bell peppers
¾ cup chopped fresh dill
1½ cups mayonnaise
1 teaspoon coarse salt
½ teaspoon freshly ground black
   pepper

Banana Birthday Cake

CAKE

½ pound (2 sticks) butter, softened

2 cups granulated sugar

2 teaspoons vanilla extract

2 eggs

4 bananas, peeled and mashed with
   a fork

2 cups unbleached white flour

⅔ cup cornstarch

½ teaspoon coarse salt

I teaspoon baking soda

I teaspoon baking powder

⅔ cup milk

I cup finely chopped walnuts

FROSTING

8 ounces cream cheese

4 tablespoons butter, softened

4 cups confectioners' sugar

½ teaspoon vanilla extract

I tablespoon grated orange peel

Preheat the oven to 350 degrees. Butter a 10-inch springform pan.

In the bowl of an electric mixer, cream the butter and sugar until light, about 5 minutes. Add the vanilla, eggs, and mashed bananas. Beat at medium speed until well blended. Add the remaining cake ingredients, and mix at low speed until well combined, about 3 minutes.

Pour the batter into the prepared pan. Smooth the top. Bake for 1¼ hours, or until a toothpick inserted in the center comes out clean. Remove from the oven and cool the cake in the pan.

To make the frosting, place all the ingredients in the electric mixer bowl and beat at medium speed until smooth, about 7 minutes.

To assemble, transfer the cooled cake to a flat cake plate. Cut the cake in half horizontally. Spread 1 cup of frosting over the bottom layer. Cover with the top layer. Frost the sides and top of the cake with the remaining frosting. Store at room temperature until ready to serve.

YIELD: 12 SERVINGS.

INFORMAL BUFFET DINNER
FOR TWENTY

This is a terrific buffet for one of those spring evenings when all the doors are open, and your guests are free to serve themselves whenever they wish and eat either inside or out. I prepared this meal the same day as my party, and laid the food out on my butcher-block counter in the kitchen. I filled some large pitchers with lilac branches two days before the party, so they would be just beginning to bloom. I passed the Green Onion Dip once, then placed it in a conspicuous spot where everyone had easy access. Detlef, my husband, lit a fire in the fireplace halfway through the evening as the warm air started to chill, and our friends wandered inside and clustered around the hearth where they helped themselves to a dessert made from rhubarb plucked from our own garden that very morning.

Even though we had 20 friends, the gathering was casual, intimate, and cozy. Here are some suggestions on how to manage this party on your own.

The Green Onion Dip can be made the night before, covered, and refrigerated. The baby carrots could be peeled then, too, and refrigerated overnight in a container of ice water.

The Jambalaya can be prepared the day before, and stored,

BABY CARROTS WITH
GREEN ONION DIP

JAMBALAYA
SALAD OF SPRING GREENS
CRUSTY FRENCH BREAD

RHUBARB CRISP WITH
WHIPPED CREAM

covered, in the refrigerator. An hour before your guests arrive, scoop the Jambalaya into a large oval casserole, cover with foil, and pop it into a preheated 350-degree oven for 40 minutes. It should be served hot.

The salad greens can be washed, dried, wrapped, and stored in the refrigerator the day before. Make the simple dressing at the last minute, and just before you place the salad on the buffet table, drizzle it with the dressing and toss to blend.

The Rhubarb Crisp can also be prepared the day before the party and baked just before serving. It's a mouth-wateringly delicious dessert that I enjoy warm, with a mound of chilled whipped cream on top.

Baby Carrots with Green Onion Dip

This particular dip is marvelous any time of the year. And it goes beautifully with almost any fresh vegetable.

GREEN ONION DIP

1 tablespoon minced garlic

8 scallion greens chopped, or 2 cups chopped chives

1 teaspoon coarse salt

½ teaspoon Tabasco

2 cups sour cream

2 cups mayonnaise

¾ pound (1 head) chicory

5 pounds baby carrots (12 to 14 count per pound), peeled, with 1 inch of the greens left on

To make the dip, place the garlic and scallion greens in the bowl of a food processor fitted with a steel blade. Purée for 10 seconds. Scrape down the sides of the bowl, and pulse 5 times. Add the remaining ingredients, and process 5 seconds, just to blend. Transfer the dip to a serving bowl, and place in the center of a platter lined with chicory leaves, surrounded by the baby carrots.

YIELD: 5 TO 6 CUPS.

Jambalaya

Gratifyingly savory, yet light, and so easy to eat. We serve this dish often to large gatherings, finding it to be a natural crowd pleaser.

Brown the bacon in a large skillet. Transfer the pieces to a small bowl. Add the onions, green peppers, and garlic to the same skillet, and sauté for 5 minutes in the bacon fat, until the onions are transparent. Stir in the thyme, salt, pepper, tomatoes, rice, stock, ham, and sausages. Cover, and bring to a boil. Reduce the heat, and simmer for about 20 minutes, until the rice is cooked almost through. Add the shrimp by pushing them into the rice, and continue to simmer, covered, until the shrimp are pink, about 5 to 10 minutes.

Stir in the bacon and the parsley, and serve.

YIELD: 24 SERVINGS.

1½ pounds bacon, coarsely chopped
3 cups chopped onions
12 cups (10 medium) chopped green bell peppers
¼ cup minced garlic
2 tablespoons chopped fresh thyme leaves, or 2 teaspoons dried
1 tablespoon coarse salt
2 teaspoons freshly ground black pepper
6 cups chopped fresh tomatoes, or drained canned tomatoes
6 cups long-grain white rice
9 cups chicken stock (page 8)
2 pounds smoked ham, coarsely chopped
4 pounds cooked hot or sweet sausages, sliced into rounds
7 pounds shrimp, peeled and deveined
⅓ cup chopped fresh parsley

Salad of Spring Greens

Made with tender red lettuce, blended with tangy sorrel, peppery spinach, and aromatic basil and mint, this salad holds up beautifully to any strongly flavored dish such as Jambalaya.

2¼ pounds (3 heads) red-leaf lettuce
½ pound (4 cups loosely packed) young sorrel leaves
½ pound (4 cups loosely packed) young spinach leaves
2 cups loosely packed mint leaves
2 cups loosely packed basil leaves

DRESSING

3 teaspoons Dijon mustard
¼ cup tarragon vinegar
¾ cup extra-virgin olive oil
1½ teaspoons coarse salt
1½ teaspoons freshly ground black pepper
6 hard-boiled egg yolks

Wash and spin-dry all the greens, then place them in a large salad bowl. Place the dressing ingredients, except for the egg yolks, in the bowl of a food processor fitted with a steel blade. Process for 10 seconds. Pour the dressing over the greens. Mash the egg yolks with a fork, and sprinkle them over the salad. Toss gently, and place on the buffet.

YIELD: 20 TO 24 SERVINGS.

Rhubarb Crisp with Whipped Cream

The first spring crop of tart, fresh rhubarb, baked into a scrumptious dessert, covered with a crispy, caramelized topping, and served with a dollop of sweetened whipped cream.

Preheat the oven to 375 degrees. Butter two 6-quart shallow casseroles with 2-inch sides.

Combine the rhubarb, sugar, flour, and cinnamon in a large mixing bowl. Divide the rhubarb mixture evenly between the casseroles. Combine the topping ingredients in a second mixing bowl. Sprinkle evenly over the 2 casseroles.

Bake for 35 to 40 minutes, until the rhubarb is tender and the topping is crisp.

Whip together the heavy cream, vanilla, and sugar until soft peaks hold. Refrigerate until ready to serve.

Serve the crisp warm or at room temperature, with the whipped cream on the side.

YIELD: 20 TO 24 SERVINGS.

4 pounds (16 cups) rhubarb, trimmed and cut into ¾-inch cubes
4 cups granulated sugar
1 cup unbleached white flour
1½ teaspoons cinnamon

TOPPING

4 cups unbleached white flour
4 cups dark brown sugar
2 cups rolled oats
1 pound (4 sticks) butter, melted and cooled

4 cups heavy cream
1 teaspoon vanilla extract
¼ cup granulated sugar

ANNIVERSARY BRUNCH
FOR SIXTEEN

SEA BREEZES

PROSCIUTTO AND
PARMESAN SOUFFLÉ

BRAISED ARTICHOKES

FRESH PAPAYA WITH LIME

BUTTER KUCHEN

VIENNESE COFFEE

An informal midday gathering with an invigorating menu that satisfies, but isn't too filling—something savory, something sweet—and above all, recipes that are easy to follow; these were the prerequisites for an anniversary menu I planned for a dear friend of ours who wanted to prepare the party all on her own.

When Detlef and I arrived, we were offered delightful Sea Breezes and lead out to the patio where the buffet had been set up. On either side of the table were crockery bowls filled with brilliant red tulips that had come from her garden.

The kitchen was so close that I had to peek inside. My friend looked very happy . . . all her work was finished. The Prosciutto and Parmesan Soufflé was in the oven. The artichokes were braised and garnished. Perfectly ripe papaya slices were arranged in a sunburst pattern on one of her prettiest trays, and in the center was a mound of green lime wedges. Next to that was the freshly baked Butter Kuchen. All that was left to make was the coffee, and that could come much later.

An effortless menu.

Make the Butter Kuchen earlier in the day. It's a great, bready cake to serve for breakfast or brunch, and is equally nice around tea time. Not too sweet, yet substantially satisfying.

The artichokes can be cleaned earlier in the day, and braised in no time at all. The papayas should be sliced earlier too, then sprinkled with lemon juice and covered to keep them fresh. Save the soufflés for last. Their assembly isn't complicated; just pop them in the oven as your guests arrive. They should be piping hot, and the last dish you bring to the buffet table.

The Viennese coffee is a perfect finale—richly brewed and topped with a frothy crown.

Sea Breezes

Combine the ingredients in a pitcher. Stir to blend.

To serve, pour the Sea Breezes into 10-ounce glasses filled with ice.

2 cups vodka
4 cups cranberry juice
4 cups grapefruit juice
4 cups seltzer

YIELD: 16 SERVINGS.

Prosciutto and Parmesan Soufflé

Preheat the oven to 375 degrees.

Butter the insides of two 4-quart shallow casseroles, each 2 inches deep. Divide ¾ cup Parmesan between the buttered casseroles, rotating them to distribute the cheese evenly over the bottoms and sides of each.

Melt the butter in a saucepan. Stir in the flour and blend well. Whisk in the hot milk until smooth, then switch to a wooden spoon and stir until the mixture thickens. Transfer to a large mixing bowl. Stir in the egg yolks, remaining Parmesan, prosciutto, chives, salt, and pepper; set aside.

Whip the egg whites in the bowl of an electric mixer until firm peaks hold. Fold them into the soufflé mixture. Blend just until the whites are incorporated but not deflated.

Divide the soufflé mixture between the two casseroles, smooth the tops, and bake for 30 minutes.

Transfer the casseroles directly from the oven to the buffet table.

3¾ cups Parmesan cheese
12 tablespoons (1½ sticks) butter
¾ cup unbleached white flour
4½ cups hot milk
18 eggs, separated
2 cups (8 ounces) finely chopped prosciutto or smoked ham
1 cup finely chopped chives or scallion greens
2 teaspoons coarse salt
¾ teaspoon freshly ground black pepper

YIELD: 16 SERVINGS.

Braised Artichokes

Chop whatever leftovers you have into a salad the next day. It's superb!

12 to 13 pounds (about 24) fresh
    artichokes, trimmed, quartered, and
    chokes removed
3 tablespoons olive oil
2 teaspoons minced garlic
1 cup dry white wine
1 cup chicken stock (page 8)
1 teaspoon coarse salt
½ teaspoon freshly ground black
    pepper
½ cup finely chopped fresh parsley

In a large sauté pan, sauté the artichokes in the olive oil over medium heat for 5 minutes. Gently shake the pan a few times.

Add the garlic, wine, chicken stock, salt, and pepper. Bring to a boil. Cover, and simmer over low heat for 20 to 25 minutes, or until the artichokes are tender when pierced with a sharp knife.

Transfer the artichokes to a serving bowl, sprinkle with the parsley, and place on the buffet table. Serve hot.

YIELD: 16 SERVINGS.

Fresh Papaya with Lime

6 papayas, peeled, seeded, and thinly
    sliced
4 limes, cut into 6 wedges each

When shopping for papayas, look for ones that are slightly soft to the touch and show no sign of green. Their color should be rich, yellow orange.

Arrange the slices on a pretty platter in a starburst pattern. Mound the green lime wedges in the center.

YIELD: 16 SERVINGS.

Butter Kuchen

In the bowl of an electric mixer, cream until light 8 table-spoons of butter, ½ cup of sugar, and the salt. Add the eggs and grated lemon peel. Beat well to blend. Add the milk and yeast, and set aside for 5 minutes, until the yeast softens.

Add 2 cups of flour, and beat at low speed for 5 minutes. Beat in another 2 cups flour.

In a small bowl, toss the raisins with 2 tablespoons flour, and add this to the dough mixture, which should be quite sticky.

Cover the bowl with a kitchen towel and let rise in a warm place for 1 hour.

Spread the dough evenly onto an 18 x 12-inch buttered baking sheet. Cut the remaining butter into small pieces, and press lightly into the dough. Sprinkle the remaining sugar evenly over the top. Let rise in a warm place for 45 minutes.

Place the kuchen in a cold oven. Turn the oven to 350 degrees, and bake 25 to 30 minutes. Serve warm, or at room temperature.

YIELD: 16 TO 20 SERVINGS.

14 tablespoons (1¾ sticks) butter
1 cup sugar
½ teaspoon coarse salt
3 eggs
1½ teaspoons grated lemon peel
1½ cups warm milk
1½ tablespoons active dry yeast
4 cups plus 2 tablespoons unbleached
    white flour
¾ cup raisins

Viennese Coffee

¾ pound (3½ cups) Viennese roast
   coffee, ground for espresso
2 cups heavy cream
⅓ cup sugar
2 tablespoons cocoa powder

Prepare the coffee in a drip-style coffee maker. If using an 8 to 10-cup coffee maker, you will need to make the coffee in 2 batches, keeping the first batch warm in a stainless steel pot over very low heat while preparing the second batch.

Whip the heavy cream with the sugar until soft peaks hold.

To serve, fill sixteen 8-ounce coffee cups three-quarters full of hot coffee. Float 1 heaping tablespoon of whipped cream on top of each cup, and dust the whipped cream with cocoa powder, dividing it evenly among all 16 cups. Serve immediately.

YIELD: 16 CUPS.

MOTHER'S DAY DINNER
FOR EIGHT

Chicken Burgers were chosen for this menu by popular demand. Simple to make and delicious, these marvelous burgers—served with a scoop of Lemon Chutney—are simply out of this world. The burgers can be assembled and shaped 1 day ahead. Store them, covered, in the refrigerator. One hour before you wish to serve them, sauté the burgers, transfer them to a roasting pan, and bake until cooked through.

The Lemon Cookies can be baked the day before and stored at room temperature in an airtight container.

The Avocado Mousse, Warm Potato Salad, and Berries and Cream should be made the day of the party. Cover and refrigerate the mousse, and store the potato salad, covered, at room temperature until ready to serve.

AVOCADO MOUSSE WITH
TORTILLA CHIPS

CHICKEN BURGERS

LEMON CHUTNEY

MÂCHE WITH SHALLOT
DRESSING

WARM POTATO SALAD

BERRIES AND CREAM

LEMON RAISIN COOKIES

Avocado Mousse with Tortilla Chips

This creamy mousse is also excellent with bagel or pita chips.

1 teaspoon chopped garlic
¼ cup fresh coriander
2 ripe avocados, peeled and pitted
1 teaspoon coarse salt
½ teaspoon freshly ground black
　　pepper
½ cup heavy cream
½ cup chopped red Spanish onion
1 sprig fresh parsley
½ pound tortilla chips

Purée the garlic and coriander in the bowl of a food processor fitted with a steel blade. Add the avocados, salt, and pepper. Process until completely smooth.

Whip the cream until soft peaks hold. Fold the avocado purée into the cream. Transfer to a small serving bowl, sprinkle with the chopped onion, and garnish with the parsley. Refrigerate, covered, until ready to serve, but no more than 2 hours. Serve with the tortilla chips in a basket on the side.

YIELD: 3 CUPS.

Chicken Burgers

1 cup minced onions
2 tablespoons butter
2 pounds boneless and skinless chicken
　　breasts, coarsely ground in a food
　　processor
2 eggs
¼ cup heavy cream
¼ cup bread crumbs
1 tablespoon coarse salt
1 teaspoon freshly ground black pepper
1 tablespoon fresh thyme leaves, or
　　1 teaspoon dried
2 tablespoons chopped fresh parsley
½ cup coarse cornmeal
2 tablespoons butter
2 tablespoon olive oil
12 sprigs fresh parsley

Preheat the oven to 375 degrees.

Sauté the onion in the butter for 8 minutes, or until transparent. Place the ground chicken in a medium-size bowl. Add the sautéed onion, eggs, heavy cream, bread crumbs, salt, pepper, thyme, and parsley. Mix well. Using your hands, shape into 10 hamburger-size patties. Coat each patty with cornmeal.

Heat the butter and olive oil in a large sauté pan over medium heat, brown the patties 4 minutes on each side, then place in a roasting pan, cover, and bake for 25 minutes. Transfer to a serving platter, and garnish with the fresh parsley sprigs.

YIELD: 10 BURGERS.

Lemon Chutney

Combine all the ingredients in a saucepan, and bring to a rolling boil. Reduce the heat and simmer, uncovered, for 1 hour. Uncover, turn up the heat, and, stirring often, boil hard for another 30 minutes, or until thickened. Allow to cool to room temperature, then cover and store in the refrigerator. The chutney will last up to 2 months.

YIELD: ABOUT 10 CUPS.

3 cups peeled and chopped green apples
6 cups thinly sliced and pitted lemons
3 cups golden or dark raisins
3 cups chopped onions
3 cups granulated sugar
4½ cups cider vinegar
½ cup minced fresh gingerroot
1½ teaspoons ground allspice
1 tablespoon coarse salt

Mâche with Shallot Dressing

Field greens are called mâche *in Europe. This is a lovely, delicate salad.*

Wash and spin-dry the mâche, and place in a salad bowl.

Combine the dressing ingredients in a screw-top jar. Just before serving, shake vigorously. Add just enough dressing to lightly coat the leaves; you may not need all of it.

NOTE: Leftover dressing will keep, covered and at room temperature, for up to 4 days.

YIELD: 8 SERVINGS.

4 quarts (2 pounds) loosely packed mâche

DRESSING
¼ cup red wine vinegar
¾ cup extra-virgin olive oil
⅓ cup (4 medium) chopped shallots
½ teaspoon salt
½ teaspoon freshly ground black pepper
½ teaspoon sugar

Warm Potato Salad

4 pounds small red new potatoes

1 pound asparagus, peeled and cut into
1-inch pieces

1 medium red onion, cut into thin half-
moon slices

½ cup chopped fresh parsley

3 hard-boiled eggs, sliced

DRESSING

3 anchovy fillets

1 teaspoon minced garlic

3 tablespoons white wine vinegar

⅔ cup extra-virgin olive oil

1 teaspoon coarse salt

1 teaspoon freshly ground black pepper

Place the potatoes in a heavy saucepan, cover with cold water, and bring to a boil. Reduce the heat, and simmer, covered, for 12 to 15 minutes, until tender. Drain, and set aside to cool.

Pour 1 inch of water into a 5-quart sauté pan, and bring to a boil. Blanch the asparagus for 2 minutes. Drain, and rinse under cold running water. Set aside.

Slice the potatoes and place in a salad bowl. Add the asparagus, red onion slices, parsley, and cooked eggs. Do not toss.

In the bowl of a food processor fitted with a steel blade, process the anchovy fillets and garlic for 10 seconds. Add the vinegar, olive oil, salt, and pepper. Process to blend, and pour over the salad. Toss gently to combine. Serve immediately.

YIELD: 8 SERVINGS.

Berries and Cream

Layer the berries alternately in a glass serving dish, starting with the strawberries on the bottom. The heavy cream should be poured into a pretty pitcher and served separately.

3 cups fresh strawberries
3 cups fresh raspberries
2 cups heavy cream

YIELD: 8 SERVINGS.

Lemon Raisin Cookies

To make Chocolate Chip Cookies, simply omit the raisins and add the same amount of chocolate chips.

Preheat the oven to 375 degrees.

Place the butter, margarine, and sugar in the bowl of an electric mixer and cream for about 5 minutes, until light and fluffy. Add the grated lemon peel and the eggs, and mix at low speed until well blended. Add the flour, baking soda, and raisins. Mix at low speed just to blend.

With your hands, roll 1-inch balls and place them 3 inches apart on an ungreased baking sheet. Dip a fork in cold water, and flatten the cookies slightly, making crisscross patterns on each top.

Bake 8 to 10 minutes, or until the edges are light brown. Remove from the oven and cool for 5 minutes. Transfer the cookies to a pretty plate.

NOTE: The cookies will last up to 5 days when stored in an airtight container.

¼ pound (1 stick) butter, softened
¼ pound margarine, softened
1½ cups sugar
1½ teaspoons grated lemon peel
2 eggs
3½ cups unbleached white flour
2 teaspoons baking soda
2 cups raisins

YIELD: 50 COOKIES.

FATHER'S DAY DINNER
FOR EIGHT

BROCCOLI FLORETS WITH
CLAM DIP

SPARERIBS WITH
PLUM BASTING SAUCE

WHITE BEAN SALAD

SPINACH SALAD WITH
GARLIC CROUTONS

CHOCOLATE CHOCOLATE CAKE

I was looking through our photo albums recently and decided I had to include this recipe. The most precious picture was of my two children, then eight and nine, elbow-deep in a bowl of chocolate cake batter, intense and earnest expressions on both their young faces as they tried to scrape as much batter as possible into the cake pans. Scanning the photo, I could see batter not only on them, but on the table, a bit on the chair, and a lot on the dog.

I'm not advising that your eight-year-old make this entire dinner for Father's Day, yet it is relatively uncomplicated, and certainly an eight-year-old can help with the Clam Dip, frost the cake, wash and dry the spinach, and maybe even turn the ribs on the grill.

My family adores these barbecued spareribs. The sweet and spicy sauce is exquisite and can be made up to a week ahead and refrigerated.

The Chocolate Chocolate Cake should be made the day before, as well as the easy-as-pie Clam Dip. The cake need not be refrigerated, but the Clam Dip needs to be covered and chilled overnight. You'll need to soak the dry beans overnight as well. Frost the cake and prepare the White Bean Salad the morning of the party.

The broccoli can be divided into florets the night before, but should be blanched on the day of the party. A half hour before the meal, reheat the finished potatoes in a preheated 350-degree oven.

Everything else will take a matter of minutes, and can be easily managed just before you sit down to eat.

Broccoli Florets with Clam Dip

The Clam Dip should be made enough in advance so that it can be refrigerated for at least 3 hours before serving. This recipe can be made any time of the year and served as a dipping sauce for any type of vegetable.

Drop the broccoli florets into 1 inch of boiling water. Toss for 1 minute. Drain, and immediately run under cold water to stop the cooking process. Cover, and refrigerate until ready to serve.

Melt the butter in a medium sauté pan over low heat. Add the onions, and sauté for 5 minutes, until transparent. Add the garlic, and sauté 1 minute more. Add the wine and clams. Bring to a boil, reduce the heat, and simmer, covered, for 5 minutes. Remove from the heat and set aside to cool. Cover and refrigerate for at least 3 hours.

Drain the clam mixture, discarding the liquid. Combine the clam mixture with the mayonnaise, sour cream, scallions, and cayenne. Adjust seasoning to taste.

Arrange the florets in a basket, with the Clam Dip in a serving dish in the middle.

YIELD: 2¾ CUPS DIP, APPROXIMATELY 8 CUPS FLORETS.

2 pounds broccoli, cut into florets
(8 cups)

CLAM DIP

2 tablespoons butter
1 cup finely chopped onions
2 tablespoons minced garlic
¼ cup dry white wine
1 pint (2 cups) chopped raw clams,
with their juices
1 cup mayonnaise
1 cup sour cream
¼ cup finely chopped scallions, green
part only
½ teaspoon cayenne
Salt, if needed

Spareribs with Plum Basting Sauce

A fabulous sweet and savory sauce, scented with fresh herbs and enlivened with a touch of chili powder and red pepper flakes. It's my family's favorite.

2 cups finely chopped fresh Italian
    prune plums
2½ cups finely chopped tomatoes
1 cup finely chopped onions
¼ cup minced garlic
1 cup apple cider vinegar
1 cup packed dark brown sugar
1 cup chicken stock
2 teaspoons chili powder
2 teaspoons red pepper flakes
2 teaspoons freshly ground black
    pepper
2 teaspoons ground cumin
1 teaspoon ground coriander
1 tablespoon coarse salt
2 tablespoons fresh rosemary leaves
½ cup Dijon mustard
12 pounds pork baby back ribs
8 large sprigs fresh rosemary

Combine all the ingredients except the ribs and rosemary sprigs in a large heavy saucepan. Bring the mixture to a boil. Reduce the heat and simmer, uncovered, for 45 minutes, stirring occasionally to prevent burning. Remove from the heat, and cool to room temperature. Store the plum sauce in the refrigerator for at least 24 hours or up to 1 week, to blend the flavors.

The ribs can be grilled outdoors over medium-hot coals, or under the broiler 4 inches from the heat source. Grill or broil the ribs for a total of 30 minutes; during the first 10 minutes, turn them once, then baste and grill for 10 more minutes, repeat the basting on both sides, and grill them the final 10 minutes.

Cut the ribs into serving-size pieces and arrange them on a large platter. Garnish with the fresh rosemary sprigs.

YIELD: 8 SERVINGS.

White Bean Salad

This is a marvelous side dish that complements any grilled fish or meat, especially veal chops.

Soak the beans in cold water overnight.

Discard the soaking liquid, and place the beans and the other ingredients for cooking them in a 6-quart pot. Add enough cold water to fill the pot half full. Bring to a boil. Simmer 1 to 1½ hours, until the beans are tender. Drain and discard the cooking liquid, onion, carrot, celery, and bacon.

Combine the dressing ingredients in a screw-top jar. Shake vigorously.

To make the salad, transfer the cooked beans to a serving bowl. Add the green pepper, sliced onion, and fresh mint. Pour the dressing over the beans and toss to blend. Serve at room temperature.

YIELD: 8 SERVINGS.

1 pound dried Great Northern beans
1 medium onion, quartered
1 carrot, quartered
1 stalk celery, quartered
1 small ham bone, or ¼ pound bacon
1 garlic clove, crushed

DRESSING

¾ cup olive oil
¼ cup white wine vinegar
½ teaspoon sugar
1 clove garlic crushed with 1 teaspoon
    coarse salt
1 teaspoon freshly ground black pepper

1¼ cups coarsely chopped green bell
    pepper
1 medium onion, cut into thin
    half-moon slices
1½ cups chopped and loosely packed
    fresh mint leaves

Spinach Salad with Garlic Croutons

3 tablespoons sesame seeds
2½ pounds fresh spinach
I large red onion, sliced into thin rings

DRESSING

¾ cup olive oil
I tablespoon toasted sesame oil
3 tablespoons lemon juice
I teaspoon salt
I teaspoon coarsely ground black
    pepper

GARLIC CROUTONS

¼ pound (I stick) salted butter,
    melted
3 cloves garlic, crushed to a purée
I baguette, cut into ½-inch-thick slices

Toss the sesame seeds in a skillet over a medium heat until lightly browned. Remove from the heat and set aside.

Thoroughly wash and dry the spinach leaves; place in a large salad bowl with the onion rings and toasted sesame seeds.

Place all the dressing ingredients in a screw-top jar. Shake vigorously, and set aside.

Preheat the oven to 350 degrees.

To make the croutons, place the slices of bread on a baking sheet in a single layer. Mix the garlic with the melted butter, and brush each top with the mixture. Bake until crisp; about 8 to 10 minutes.

When ready to serve, dress the salad and toss to coat well. Pass the croutons separately in a basket.

YIELD: 8 SERVINGS.

Chocolate Chocolate Cake

Lavishly rich, and supremely chocolatey!

Preheat the oven to 325 degrees. Butter two 9-inch spring-form pans.

In the bowl of an electric mixer, cream the butter and sugar until light. Add 1 cup of flour, the baking soda, cocoa, cinnamon, coffee, and vanilla. Beat at low speed for about 5 minutes, until fluffy. Add the remaining flour and the sour cream. Beat at low speed to blend well.

In a separate bowl, beat the egg whites until soft peaks hold. Using a rubber spatula, fold the egg whites into the chocolate batter. Pour the batter into the prepared pans, and spread evenly.

Bake 25 minutes, or until a toothpick inserted in the center comes out clean. Remove from the oven and cool in the pans.

To make the frosting, beat the butter, confectioners' sugar, cocoa, and water, until very light and spreadable.

Transfer 1 cake layer to a cake plate. Spread the top with frosting, cover with the second cake layer, and spread the remaining frosting over the top and sides of the cake.

Stored at room temperature, the cake will keep for up to 5 days.

YIELD: 10 TO 12 SERVINGS.

½ pound (2 sticks) butter, softened
2¾ cups sugar
2½ cups unbleached white flour
1 teaspoon baking soda
¾ cup Swiss or Belgian cocoa
1 teaspoon ground cinnamon
1 cup brewed coffee
2 teaspoons vanilla extract
1 cup sour cream
5 egg whites

FROSTING

4 tablespoons butter, softened
1 pound confectioners' sugar
¾ cup cocoa
½ cup water

THE BEST OF SUMMER

BUFFET DINNER IN THE BACKYARD FOR EIGHT

SUNDAY BRUNCH FOR SIX

SATURDAY DINNER FOR TWELVE

FRIDAY DINNER FOR EIGHT

ENGAGEMENT PARTY FOR TWENTY

WEDDING RECEPTION FOR FORTY

FOURTH OF JULY CELEBRATION FOR SIXTEEN

SUMMER DINNER FOR TWELVE

COOL SUMMER LUNCH FOR EIGHT

COCKTAIL PARTY ON THE LAWN FOR FORTY

LABOR DAY—THE LAST HURRAH! FOR SIXTEEN

Our friends and customers love to create impromptu gatherings in the summer, because of the ease and fun of entertaining during this glorious season. With an outdoor grill we acquire another kitchen. Our doors open up to include the garden as an alternate living room, our patio as another dining area. What could be more inviting than brunch under a cobalt blue sky or a barbecue dinner under the stars? Especially with a cornucopia of garden-fresh produce right at your fingertips to help turn any event into a special occasion.

Since this is the season for outdoor entertaining, you may find that your guest lists are larger than usual. In order to enjoy giving parties on a grand scale, remember that it's best to keep the preplanning and preparations as simple and straightforward as possible. The less time spent in the kitchen, the better. By the time your guests arrive, you should be free to be outside with them. Keeping this in mind, we have chosen a collection of recipes that covers an intriguing array of party possibilities. Some are casual and intimate, others larger and more daring.

If you're planning to entertain friends over a long weekend, it is very important to plan the meals and do all your shopping ahead of time. For Friday night, prepare a simple meal, so you too can unwind from the long week. Buy lots of freshly baked croissants and muffins, and on Saturday morning present them buffet-style, with loads of sweet butter, honey, and preserves. This will allow the early and late risers to eat at their leisure.

Saturday Dinner for twelve is a buffet-style menu, simple to organize and prepare and specially designed to expand in case you want to enlarge the gathering. The piece de resistance is the Berries and Cream Cake, which is so easy to make and so thoroughly delicious that you may find yourself reusing the recipe throughout the long summer months.

A pitcher of freshly squeezed orange juice, a pot of freshly brewed coffee, the morning papers, the aroma of sausages cooking in the kitchen—welcome delights to waken to on a Sunday morning. Everyone contented and relaxed. A perfect ending to a perfect weekend.

BUFFET DINNER IN THE BACKYARD
FOR EIGHT

MARINATED TURKEY BREAST
WITH CORIANDER-LIME
SAUCE

MOZZARELLA, TOMATOES,
AND ONIONS

BLACK BEAN SALAD

PEACH PIE
VANILLA ICE CREAM

Whether you have a small city terrace, a postage-stamp-size backyard, or plan to entertain eight friends on the deck of your boat, this is an ideally compact menu. We created a variation of this (expanding it to serve twenty-four guests), and prepared the party for a family who lived in Sag Harbor, a charming, historic village on Long Island. Drinks were served on the porch, dinner on tables set up on the grass, and dessert followed dancing on the patio.

Practically everything on the menu can be prepared a day ahead; it can also be pulled together 2 hours before your party. The choice will be up to you.

Marinate the turkey breasts the night before, and refrigerate, or place them in the marinade and keep at room temperature 2 hours before your guests arrive.

The Coriander-Lime Sauce and Vanilla Ice Cream can be prepared the day before, or a couple of hours before, your party begins. You will only have the initial stages of the ice cream to worry about, an ice cream machine will do the rest.

The Black Bean Salad can be made and dressed the day before and refrigerated, or it can be assembled the same day as the party and served at room temperature.

Mozzarella, Tomatoes, and Onions takes minutes to prepare, and can be whipped together as your friends are having their first drink.

The pastry for the pie can be prepared the day before and stored in the refrigerator, but bake the pie the morning of the party, or wait until late afternoon, when the weather cools a little. Some people worry about the juicy overflow that automatically comes with baking fresh fruit pies. Line the bottom of the oven with some foil; don't place a baking sheet under the pie plate because this will retard the baking process. Hot air needs to flow freely around the pie, so it cooks evenly and browns to perfection.

Marinated Turkey Breast with Coriander-Lime Sauce

This tangy, pungent sauce is a perfect match for the delicate taste of turkey.

Cut the meat off the bone and remove the skin, or if you prefer, ask your butcher to do it for you. Combine the marinade ingredients in a large glass or earthenware casserole, and stir to blend well. Add the halved turkey breast, turning both pieces to coat well on both sides. Cover, and marinate in the refrigerator for 12 hours or overnight.

To make the coriander lime sauce, place all the ingredients except the peanut oil in the bowl of a food processor fitted with a steel blade. Process for a few seconds. With the motor running, add the peanut oil in droplets until the mixture is thick, then add the rest of the oil in a thin stream. If the sauce is too thick, add a bit more lime juice.

Preheat the broiler for 10 minutes.

Preheat the oven to 375 degrees. If your oven and broiler operate on one dial, you will need to lower the temperature to 375 degrees after the initial broiling is completed.

Transfer the turkey to a shallow roasting pan. Broil 2 inches from the heat source for about 10 minutes, or until nicely browned. Pour the marinade over the turkey breast, place in the oven, and roast for about 35 minutes, or until the juices run clear when a knife is inserted in the center. Remove from the oven, and cool for 10 minutes to settle the juices. Slice the turkey and arrange the pieces on a platter garnished with the flat-leaf parsley. Serve the sauce on the side.

YIELD: 8 TO 10 SERVINGS, 2½ CUPS SAUCE.

1 turkey breast, approximately 10 pounds, bone in

MARINADE

¼ cup toasted sesame oil
3 tablespoons lemon juice
¼ cup soy sauce
½ cup white wine
4 teaspoons minced garlic
1 tablespoon fresh thyme leaves, or 1 teaspoon dried
1 teaspoon hot red pepper flakes

CORIANDER-LIME SAUCE

4 egg yolks
2 teaspoons minced garlic
1½ tablespoons seeded and finely chopped jalapeño peppers
1½ teaspoons Dijon mustard
1 tablespoon soy sauce
3 tablespoons lime juice
½ teaspoon salt
2 cups fresh coriander leaves
2½ cups peanut oil
½ teaspoon coarse salt

10 sprigs flat-leaf parsley

Mozzarella, Tomatoes, and Onions

1¼ pounds fresh mozzarella cheese,
  thinly sliced
3 pounds ripe tomatoes, thinly sliced
1 medium (½ pound) Spanish onion,
  sliced paper thin and separated into
  rings
2½ tablespoons red wine vinegar
2 cups loosely packed basil leaves
½ cup extra-virgin olive oil
1 teaspoon coarse salt
½ teaspoon freshly ground black
  pepper

Alternate the mozzarella and tomato slices on a serving platter. Sprinkle the onion rings over the top.

Place the vinegar and 1 cup of the basil leaves in the bowl of a food processor fitted with a steel blade. Process for 10 seconds. Add the olive oil, salt, and pepper. Process 10 seconds more.

Drizzle the dressing over the mozzarella, tomatoes, and onions. Garnish the platter with the remaining basil leaves.

YIELD: 8 SERVINGS.

Black Bean Salad

An exciting, spicy bean salad that stands up well to any meat dish, and is excellent when paired with Chicken Burgers (page 40).

1 pound dried black turtle beans
3 cups diced celery
2 red onions, sliced into thin half-moon
  rings
1½ cups (approximately 1 bunch)
  coarsely chopped, loosely packed
  fresh coriander leaves
4 teaspoons coarse salt
1½ teaspoons freshly ground black
  pepper
¼ teaspoon cayenne
2 teaspoons ground cumin

Place the beans in a large pot. Add enough cold water to cover the beans by 2 inches. Bring to a boil. Remove from the heat, cover, and soak for 1 hour.

Drain the beans and pour them back into the same pot. Add enough cold water to cover the beans by 4 inches. Bring to a boil and simmer, covered, for 1½ hours.

Drain the beans, and transfer them to a large bowl. Add the celery, onions, and fresh coriander. Sprinkle the salt, pepper, cayenne, and cumin over the beans.

To make the dressing, combine all the ingredients in a screw-top jar and shake vigorously. Pour over the beans and toss to coat.

YIELD: 8 TO 10 SERVINGS.

DRESSING

¾ cup olive oil

3 tablespoons red wine vinegar

I teaspoon minced garlic

I teaspoon Dijon mustard

Peach Pie

To make the pastry, place the flour in the bowl of a food processor fitted with a steel blade. Cut the butter and margarine into tablespoon-size pieces, and add to the flour. Pulse 5 times. With the motor running, add the lemon juice and 2 tablespoons of cold water. Process until the dough starts to cling together. Scrape the dough onto a lightly floured countertop, gather into a ball, and wrap in wax paper. Chill for 30 minutes.

To make the filling, combine the peaches, flour, sugar, nutmeg, cinnamon, and orange peel in a large bowl.

Preheat the oven to 375 degrees.

Divide the dough in half, and roll one half into an 11-inch circle. Fit the circle into a 9-inch pie plate.

Spoon the peach filling into the pie shell and dot with the butter.

Roll the remaining dough into a 10-inch round. Fit over the top of the peaches. Trim off the excess and flute the edges. Cut slits in the top to allow steam to escape.

Brush the top of the pie with the egg wash and sprinkle with sugar.

Bake 45 to 50 minutes, or until the top is golden brown. Remove from the oven, and cool for 1 hour before serving.

NOTE: Leftovers can be kept, covered, at room temperature for up to 2 days.

YIELD: 8 SERVINGS.

PASTRY

2 cups unbleached white flour

6 tablespoons cold butter

6 tablespoons cold margarine

2 tablespoons lemon juice

2 tablespoons cold water

FILLING

6 cups peeled, pitted, and sliced fresh peaches

¼ cup unbleached white flour

¾ cup sugar

¼ teaspoon freshly grated nutmeg

½ teaspoon ground cinnamon

I tablespoon grated orange peel

2 tablespoons butter, softened

I egg yolk mixed with I tablespoon heavy cream

3 tablespoons sugar

Vanilla Ice Cream

2 cups milk
¾ cup sugar
1 vanilla bean, softened at least 4
   weeks in vodka, split lengthwise
   (pages 7–8)
2 cups heavy cream

Combine the milk, sugar, and vanilla bean in a heavy saucepan. Stirring frequently, heat over a low flame until the sugar is dissolved.

Add the heavy cream, stirring to blend. Chill the mixture for 30 minutes.

Remove the vanilla bean, pour the mixture into an ice cream maker, and freeze according to the manufacturer's instructions.

NOTE: For variety, you can add ¼ teaspoon almond extract; if you love coffee ice cream, add 2 tablespoons instant espresso dissolved in 2 tablespoons hot water; and if you're a chocolate lover, add ½ cup of coarsely grated Belgian chocolate.

YIELD: 8 SERVINGS.

SUNDAY BRUNCH
FOR SIX

Think of your guests waking up to a gentle morning sun. The aroma of freshly brewed coffee filtering into their rooms, followed a moment later by the tantalizing smell of sausages being grilled. Just as their mouths begin to water, they get their first whiff of muffins baking in the oven, a perfect prelude to a Sunday Brunch.

Since this brunch is part of a long weekend of entertaining, it seems only right that it be the kind of menu that can be prepared in under 2 hours. If, however, you plan to use this menu at another time, here are some time-saving suggestions:

Bake the Blueberry–Oat Bran Muffins the day before, seal them in plastic bags overnight, and warm them 5 minutes before serving in the preheated 375-degree oven. The pie can also be baked the day before, and reheated in a 375-degree oven for 20 minutes. The salad dressing can be made then, too, but stored at room temperature.

Look over the recipes before starting, just so you can figure out your timing. This menu was devised to make your job easy, and at the same time offer a gratifyingly tasty brunch for your guests. I hope it will be one you will want to use over and over again.

SAUSAGE AND TOMATO PIE

WATERCRESS SALAD

BLUEBERRY–OAT BRAN MUFFINS

SLICED MELON

Sausage and Tomato Pie

A savory pie that will easily satisfy all your breakfast cravings.

PASTRY

1½ cups unbleached white flour

2 tablespoons cornstarch

½ teaspoon coarse salt

¼ pound (1 stick) margarine, cut into
  ½-inch pieces

1 egg yolk

2 tablespoons cold water

FILLING

5 hot Italian sausages

10 scallions, sliced

1 teaspoon minced garlic

2 cups (½ pound) grated Gruyère
  cheese

3 eggs

½ cup cottage cheese

¾ cup heavy cream

1½ teaspoons coarse salt

¼ teaspoon Tabasco

¼ teaspoon freshly ground black
  pepper

2 medium tomatoes, sliced

2 tablespoons chopped fresh parsley

2 tablespoons grated Parmesan cheese

To make the pastry, combine the flour, cornstarch, salt, and margarine in the bowl of a food processor fitted with a metal blade. Pulse 5 times. Add the egg yolk and cold water. Pulse 4 times. Turn the dough out onto a lightly floured surface and work quickly into a ball. Wrap in plastic and chill for 30 minutes.

Preheat the oven to 400 degrees.

Roll the pastry into an 11-inch circle. Fit the circle into a 9½-inch springform pan, pressing it evenly over the bottom and 1½ inches up the sides. Line the pastry with foil, and fill with dry beans. Bake 20 minutes. Remove the foil and beans and bake 5 minutes more. Remove from the oven, and set aside at room temperature until ready for filling.

To make the filling, sauté the sausages until done, about 10 minutes. Cut into bite-size pieces, and scatter evenly into the pastry shell. Sprinkle the scallions and garlic over the sausage. Cover with the grated Gruyère cheese.

Process together the eggs, cottage cheese, heavy cream, salt, Tabasco, and pepper, until well blended. Pour the mixture slowly into the pie, distributing it evenly. Layer the tomato slices on top, and sprinkle with parsley and Parmesan.

Bake 40 to 50 minutes, until the custard is set. The pie should be evenly browned and slightly puffed. Remove from the oven and cool for 15 minutes before serving.

YIELD: 6 TO 8 SERVINGS.

Watercress Salad

Nutritious and delicious. Crisp watercress, savory onions, and delectably sweet toasted pecans.

In a large skillet, lightly toss the pecans over medium heat until browned. Set aside.

Wash and spin-dry the watercress, and remove and discard the stems. Place the watercress leaves, onion, and pecans in a salad bowl.

Combine the dressing ingredients in a screw-top jar, and shake vigorously. Pour over the salad, tossing to coat.

YIELD: 6 SERVINGS.

¾ cup pecans
4 bunches watercress
1 medium onion, cut into thin half-moon slices

DRESSING

2 tablespoons lemon juice
6 tablespoons olive oil
1 tablespoon heavy cream
⅛ teaspoon Tabasco
1 teaspoon coarse salt

Blueberry—Oat Bran Muffins

We make these muffins at Loaves and Fishes every weekend by the hundreds, and within hours they are all sold. I fancy these myself. A country muffin, spiced with cardamom and cinnamon, sweetened naturally with blueberries, and enriched with oat bran. Serve them warm, with sweet butter on the side—they're unbeatable!

2½ cups unbleached white flour
½ cup oat bran
1 tablespoon baking powder
1 cup sugar
¼ teaspoon salt
2 teaspoons ground cinnamon
1 teaspoon ground cardamom
2 eggs
1 cup milk
12 tablespoons (1½ sticks) butter, melted, and slightly cooled
1½ cups fresh blueberries

Preheat the oven to 400 degrees.

Combine the dry ingredients in a large mixing bowl. Add the eggs, milk, and butter. Mix to blend, without overmixing. Fold in the blueberries.

Divide the batter among 12 paper-lined, ¾-cup muffin pan cups, and bake for 25 to 30 minutes.

YIELD: 12 MUFFINS.

SATURDAY DINNER
FOR TWELVE

If you've spent the afternoon on the beach, and you are entertaining twelve for dinner, the most pressing problem is time. The beauty of this menu is that everything can be prepared in 2 hours.

Once you have the onions, lettuce, and coriander leaves chopped, and the potatoes peeled and diced, the Coriander-Lettuce Soup can be made quite simply. All I ask is that you allow it to cool sufficiently before adding the cream and puréeing it in batches. It has nothing to do with taste—it's a safety precaution. This particular soup seems to retain heat longer than most others, and instead of dealing with boiling hot liquid it would seem more prudent to get on with the rest of the meal before returning to the soup. If you prefer to serve it cold, make the soup early in the day, cover, and refrigerate it until you're ready to purée it. This last stage will go at a lightning speed.

The salmon steaks should only marinate for 1 hour before grilling.

The cucumber relish takes only minutes.

The Baked New Potatoes and Yellow Peppers is quickly assembled, and the baking time is only 30 to 35 minutes. Time it so that this baked mélange is the last item finished and still piping hot when served.

If you have the time, the Berries and Cream Cake layers can be made the day before the party and stored in their pans at room temperature, covered with plastic wrap. They can also be made up to 4 weeks ahead and frozen.

CORIANDER-LETTUCE SOUP
WITH PITA TRIANGLES

GRILLED PEPPER-CRUSTED
SALMON STEAKS
WITH CUCUMBER RELISH

BAKED NEW POTATOES AND
YELLOW PEPPERS

BERRIES AND CREAM CAKE

Coriander-Lettuce Soup with Pita Triangles

A fragile green color, this flavorsome soup is hearty and substantial when served hot, yet refreshing and surprisingly light when served cold.

6 tablespoons butter

4 cups chopped onions

4 teaspoons minced garlic

3½ cups peeled and diced potatoes

8 cups chicken stock (page 8)

1½ teaspoons coarse salt

½ teaspoon freshly ground black pepper

¼ teaspoon Tabasco

16 cups (3 large heads) coarsely chopped Boston lettuce, loosely packed

2½ cups coarsely chopped coriander leaves, plus 12 whole leaves for garnish

¾ cup heavy cream

4 large pita breads

Melt the butter in a large saucepan. Add the onions, and sauté over low heat without browning for about 5 minutes. Add the garlic, potatoes, chicken stock, salt, pepper, and Tabasco. Bring the mixture to a boil, and simmer, covered, for 20 minutes.

Add the lettuce and coriander, stirring only until the leaves are wilted. Remove from the heat and cool the soup for about 1 hour, uncovered. Purée the soup in batches in a blender, about 5 minutes per batch to make certain the ingredients don't separate; add some cream to each batch.

To make the pita triangles, cut each pita bread into 8 wedges, pie fashion. Place the pieces on a baking sheet, and toast in the oven for 15 minutes, or until the edges are slightly browned.

To serve the soup cold, chill it in the refrigerator for at least 4 hours. To serve hot, return the soup to the saucepan and reheat over medium heat until it begins to boil. Ladle into cups or soup bowls, and garnish with whole coriander leaves. Serve with the toasted pita triangles on the side.

YIELD: 12 SERVINGS.

Grilled Pepper-Crusted Salmon Steaks with Cucumber Relish

Encrusted with freshly ground pepper, these salmon steaks are blackened over an open grill, masking the pink, juicy meat inside. The relish is freshened with cool cucumbers and yogurt and spiced with garlic and chives.

Combine the olive oil, balsamic vinegar, salt, and thyme in a shallow, noncorrodible casserole. Add the salmon, and spoon the mixture over the steaks. Let salmon marinate at room temperature for 1 to 2 hours, turning once or twice.

Make the relish while the salmon is marinating. Wash and dry the cucumbers, and, leaving the skin on, slice them very thin and place in a colander. Sprinkle 2 teaspoons of salt over the cucumbers, and let stand at room temperature for 15 minutes. Drain off all the liquid. In a serving bowl, combine 2 teaspoons salt, the yogurt, chives, and garlic. Mix thoroughly, add the cucumber slices, and chill for 1 hour.

Heat the grill for approximately 50 to 60 minutes, until the coals are white.

Lift the salmon steaks out of the marinade. Drizzle 1 tablespoon of marinade on each steak, then press the pepper lightly into both sides of the fish.

Grill the steaks approximately 5 minutes on each side, or until just done. Place on 12 warm dinner plates. Pass the relish separately.

1 cup olive oil
3 tablespoons balsamic vinegar
2 teaspoons coarse salt
¼ cup fresh thyme leaves, or
   1 tablespoon dried
Twelve 1¼-inch-thick fresh salmon
   steaks (about 8 ounces each)

RELISH

4 seedless cucumbers
4 teaspoons coarse salt
3 cups plain yogurt
1 cup chopped fresh chives
2 teaspoons minced garlic

¾ cup coarsely ground black pepper

YIELD: 12 SERVINGS, 4 CUPS OF RELISH.

Baked New Potatoes and Yellow Peppers

The potatoes become crusty brown; the yellow peppers brown, soften, and retain their sweetness.

20 medium new potatoes, cut into bite-size pieces
6 yellow peppers, quartered, seeds discarded
1 cup extra-virgin olive oil
1 tablespoon sesame oil
Coarse salt
½ cup finely chopped parsley

Preheat the oven to 400 degrees.

Place the potato pieces in a roasting pan. Place the pepper slices, cut side up, in a second roasting pan.

Combine the oils, and drizzle half over the potatoes and half over the peppers. Sprinkle with coarse salt.

Roast the potatoes for 30 to 35 minutes, and the peppers for 20 to 25 minutes, or until tender. Arrange the potatoes and peppers on a platter, sprinkle with parsley, and serve.

YIELD: 12 SERVINGS.

Berries and Cream Cake

In Germany this is called Blitz Torte, *which means "lightning cake"—a perfect description of how easily it can be assembled and made. Some feel this may also describe how quickly it melts in your mouth, and how quickly it disappears off your guests' plates.*

Preheat the oven to 350 degrees. Lightly butter the bottoms of two 9-inch springform pans.

Using an electric mixer, cream together the butter and ½ cup of the sugar until light. Add the 4 egg yolks and blend thoroughly. Add the flour, cornstarch, baking powder, milk, and 1 teaspoon of vanilla extract. Stir to combine well. Divide the batter evenly between the prepared pans, so that it just covers the bottoms.

In a clean bowl, beat the 4 egg whites until soft peaks hold. Still beating, slowly add 1 cup of sugar and 1 teaspoon vanilla. Stir to blend. Spread half the egg white mixture on top of each unbaked cake layer. Sprinkle with the almonds. Bake 25 minutes, or until evenly browned. Remove from the oven, and cool at room temperature uncovered in their pans for at least 3 hours or up to 1 day.

To make the filling, pour the heavy cream into the clean bowl of an electric mixer. Add the sugar and vanilla. Beat at high speed until soft peaks hold.

To assemble the cake, place one cake layer, meringue-side down, on a cake plate. Spread evenly with whipped cream. Top the layer with the berries of your choice. Place the second layer on top of the berries, meringue-side up.

YIELD: 12 SERVINGS.

BLITZ TORTE

¼ pound (1 stick) butter
1½ cups sugar
4 eggs, separated
¾ cup unbleached white flour
¼ cup cornstarch
1½ teaspoons baking powder
2 tablespoons milk
2 teaspoons vanilla extract
¾ cup sliced almonds

FILLING

1 cup heavy cream
1 tablespoon confectioners' sugar
¼ teaspoon vanilla extract
1 pint fresh raspberries or strawberries

FRIDAY DINNER
FOR EIGHT

MEXICAN BOW TIES

SLICED SMOKED
CHICKEN BREASTS AND
AVOCADO
WITH MUSTARD SAUCE

GREEN BEANS WITH
CRÈME FRAÎCHE
AND HAZELNUTS

OATMEAL BROWNIES

The Mexican Bow Ties, Mustard Sauce, and Oatmeal Brownies can all be made the morning of the party. The Smoked Chicken and Avocado can be sliced earlier in the day; however, be sure to dip the avocado slices into a mixture of 2 cups cold water and 3 tablespoons lemon juice. This will keep them from turning brown.

The green beans should be prepared no more than an hour ahead since they are best served slightly warm.

And that's it. The dinner is easy as pie!

Mexican Bow Ties

Dressed with a salsa that has the undeniable bite of jalapeño peppers, and refined by a generous helping of fresh coriander, this refreshing dish is delicious, served hot or at room temperature.

Drop the bow-tie pasta into boiling water and simmer for about 12 minutes.

While the pasta is cooking, combine the remaining ingredients in a large serving bowl.

When the pasta is done, drain and add to the bowl. Mix well with sauce. Serve either hot or at room temperature.

YIELD: 8 TO 10 SERVINGS.

2 pounds dry farfalle (medium-size
    bow-tie pasta)
I cup finely chopped onions
2½ cups coarsely chopped green bell
    peppers
2½ cups coarsely chopped tomatoes
4 teaspoons minced garlic
3 tablespoons minced jalapeño peppers
I cup grated Parmesan cheese
I½ cups coarsely chopped fresh
    coriander
I cup olive oil
3 tablespoons lime juice
2 teaspoons coarse salt
I teaspoon freshly ground black pepper

Sliced Smoked Chicken Breasts and Avocado with Mustard Sauce

Slice the chicken breasts on the diagonal. Pit and peel the avocados. Cut each lengthwise into 8 pieces. Arrange the chicken and avocado slices on a serving platter.

To make the sauce, combine all the ingredients in a bowl. Serve on the side.

YIELD: 8 SERVINGS.

4 whole boneless smoked chicken
    breasts, about ¾ pound each
4 ripe, rough-skinned, dark green
    avocados

MUSTARD SAUCE

¾ cup Dijon Mustard
I½ cups mayonnaise
¼ cup orange juice
I tablespoon grated orange peel
½ teaspoon freshly ground black
    pepper

Green Beans with Crème Fraîche and Hazelnuts

½ cup sliced hazelnuts
2½ pounds green beans, trimmed

DRESSING

½ cup crème fraîche (page 9)
½ cup mayonnaise
2 teaspoons Dijon mustard
1 teaspoon coarse salt
½ teaspoon freshly ground black
   pepper

Lightly toss the sliced hazelnuts in a skillet over medium heat until browned. Set aside.

Drop the beans into boiling water and simmer for 4 minutes.

Combine the dressing ingredients in a large mixing bowl. Drain the beans and add them to the dressing, tossing to coat thoroughly. Just before serving at room temperature, sprinkle with the toasted hazelnuts.

YIELD: 8 SERVINGS.

Oatmeal Brownies

From start to finish, these brownies take less than an hour to make, which is fortunate, since they go at such a rapid rate that I find myself having to replenish the supply quite frequently!

6 ounces semisweet chocolate
6 tablespoons butter
¾ cup oatmeal
⅔ cup flour
½ teaspoon baking soda
½ teaspoon coarse salt
¾ cup coarsely chopped walnuts
⅓ cup light brown sugar
¼ cup granulated sugar
2 teaspoons instant espresso
2 eggs
1 teaspoon vanilla extract

Preheat the oven to 375 degrees. Butter an 8 x 8 x 2-inch baking pan.

Melt the chocolate and butter together, and set aside.

Combine the dry ingredients in a medium mixing bowl. Stir in the eggs, vanilla, and chocolate mixture.

Pour into the prepared baking pan and bake 25 minutes.

Cool in the pan, uncovered, for at least 4 hours before cutting.

Wrapped tightly in plastic and frozen, the brownies will keep for 3 months.

YIELD: 16 BROWNIES.

ENGAGEMENT PARTY
FOR TWENTY

This sumptuous buffet will work extremely well as either a lunch or a dinner—indoors or out.

Most of it, such as the Veal Roll, Peach Mousse, and Heidesand Cookies, can be prepared the day before. When shopping for the meat, ask your butcher for lean stewing veal, and cut it into approximately 1½-inch squares.

The zucchini can be sliced and stored in the refrigerator overnight, covered with a damp cloth. It's easy to blanch and dress the day of the party.

The pepper dish and the pastini should be made the same morning as the event. Also the lobsters. If you don't want to steam them yourself, ask your fishmonger to do it for you. The lobster filling should be made no more than 3 hours ahead; it's essential that it be very fresh tasting.

This menu was designed to balance varying tastes, textures, and colors. It's a gorgeous buffet presentation that is certain to please the most sophisticated palates.

SUMMER LOBSTER IN
ORANGE SAUCE

VEAL ROLL

ZUCCHINI WITH
MUSTARD VINAIGRETTE

PEPPERS WITH OLIVE OIL
AND CAPERS

PASTINI WITH CRÈME
FRAÎCHE

CHILLED PEACH MOUSSE

HEIDESAND COOKIES

Summer Lobster in Orange Sauce

Sixteen 1½-pound live lobsters
5 oranges, peeled and sectioned
3 cups coarsely chopped celery
2½ teaspoons coarse salt
1¼ teaspoons freshly ground black
  pepper

ORANGE SAUCE

3 cups mayonnaise
1½ cups sour cream
½ cup heavy cream
1½ tablespoons grated orange peel
¾ cup freshly squeezed orange juice
3 tablespoons cognac
3 tablespoons ketchup
½ cup finely chopped fresh mint leaves
½ cup minced onion
1½ cups finely chopped dill
½ teaspoon cayenne
1½ teaspoons coarse salt

Dill sprigs for garnish

Depending on the size of your pot, you will need to steam the lobsters in 3 or 4 batches. Steam each batch in 3 inches of boiling water for 12 minutes. Remove from the heat and set aside.

When the lobsters are cool enough to handle, place them on a cutting board and cut them in half, lengthwise, all the way through. Remove the meat from the accessible parts of the lobsters and place in a mixing bowl. Reserving the tail shells for garnish, cover the remaining lobster shells with a kitchen towel, and smash the covered lobsters with the broad side of a cleaver. Take the remaining lobster meat out of the shells and transfer to the mixing bowl.

Add the orange sections, celery, salt, and pepper to the lobster meat.

To make the sauce, combine all the ingredients in a mixing bowl. Pour 1½ cups of sauce over the lobster and mix well.

Arrange the tail shells, sunburst-fashion, along the outer rim of a large round serving platter. Fill each shell with lobster salad. Mound the remaining salad in the center of the platter. Garnish with fresh dill. Serve the remaining dressing on the side.

YIELD: 20 SERVINGS.

Veal Roll

This makes an excellent luncheon dish when served with a green vegetable salad topped with a mustard vinaigrette and black bread. Remember to chill the Veal Roll overnight before serving for the flavors to blend and the filling to set.

Heat the olive oil in a skillet. Add the onions, and sauté over low heat until they are transparent, about 5 minutes. Add the garlic and sauté 1 minute more. Transfer this mixture to a large bowl.

Place the mushrooms in the bowl of a food processor fitted with a steel blade. Process until fine, and add to the mixing bowl.

Process the veal and bacon in 3 or 4 batches, until finely chopped. Transfer each batch as it is ready to the mixing bowl. Add the remaining ingredients except the veal scallops and the lemon leaves. Mix with your hands until well combined.

Preheat the oven to 375 degrees.

To assemble the veal roll, flatten the scallops with a cleaver. Lay them out on a counter, overlapping to form two 12 x 16-inch rectangles. Divide the veal filling between the two rectangles, forming a sausage shape down the center of each. Fold the scallops over the filling to form rolls. Tie with cotton string at 2-inch intervals. Place both rolls in a roasting pan rubbed with olive oil.

Bake, uncovered, for 45 minutes. Cover with foil, and bake 45 minutes more.

Remove from the oven, cool, cover the pan with foil, and chill overnight. To serve, slice into ¼-inch-thick pieces (there will be about 40). Arrange on a platter, and garnish with the lemon leaves.

3 tablespoons olive oil
¾ cup finely chopped onions
3 teaspoons minced garlic
1¼ pounds fresh mushrooms
5 pounds veal, cut into
    1½ x 1½-inch chunks
6 ounces bacon
3 eggs
2 tablespoons fresh thyme leaves, or
    1 tablespoon dried
1 teaspoon ground coriander
1½ tablespoons coarse salt
1 tablespoon freshly ground black
    pepper
3 tablespoons green peppercorns,
    drained

4 pounds veal scallops
20 lemon leaves for garnish

YIELD: 20 SERVINGS.

Zucchini with Mustard Vinaigrette

7 to 8 pounds (14 to 16 small)
   zucchini, washed, dried, and cut into
   ⅛-inch rounds

MUSTARD VINAIGRETTE

½ cup red wine vinegar
1½ cups extra-virgin olive oil
¼ cup Dijon mustard
2 teaspoons coarse salt
1 teaspoon freshly ground black pepper

Place the zucchini rounds in a large salad bowl.

To make the dressing, combine the ingredients in a screw-top jar. Shake vigorously. Pour over the zucchini and toss lightly to blend.

YIELD: 20 SERVINGS.

Peppers with Olive Oil and Capers

10 yellow peppers
1 cup extra-virgin olive oil
¼ cup coarse salt
2 heads radicchio
½ cup capers
Freshly ground black pepper

Preheat the oven to 375 degrees.

Quarter the peppers lengthwise and discard the seeds and membranes. Rub a little olive oil over the bottom of a large roasting pan. Place the peppers, skin-side down, slightly overlapping in the pan. Drizzle the remaining olive oil over the peppers, and sprinkle with salt.

Roast for about 30 minutes, or until the peppers are tender. Line a large platter with a bed of radicchio leaves, and layer the pepper strips over the top. Sprinkle with capers and freshly ground black pepper.

YIELD: 20 SERVINGS.

Pastini with Crème Fraîche

This creamy side dish is great with any grilled steak or fish, and excellent with marinated turkey breasts. Pastini is best when served at room temperature.

Fill a 5-quart pot with water and bring to a boil. Plunge the pastini into the water, and cook according to the package instructions, until just tender. Drain in a colander, and transfer to a large serving bowl. Add the remaining ingredients and toss to blend.

Serve at room temperature.

2 pounds dried pastini
4 cups crème fraîche (page 9)
4 cups chopped scallions
1 tablespoon plus 1 teaspoon coarse salt
2 teaspoons freshly ground black pepper

YIELD: 20 TO 24 SERVINGS.

Chilled Peach Mousse

This deliciously refreshing dessert needs to chill for 2 hours before serving.

Peel, pit, and coarsely chop the peaches. Place them in the bowl of a food processor fitted with a steel blade. Add the lemon juice, confectioners' sugar, and brandy. Purée until smooth, and transfer to a large mixing bowl.

In an electric mixer, beat the egg whites until soft peaks hold. Fold into the peach purée. Using the same beater and bowl, whip 5 cups of heavy cream until soft peaks hold. Fold the whipped cream into the peach mixture.

Spoon the mousse into two 3-quart, freezer-proof bowls. Cover with plastic wrap, and freeze.

Two hours before serving time, beat the remaining cup of heavy cream with the sugar until soft peaks hold. Garnish the frozen mousse with the cream. Store the mousse in the refrigerator for 2 hours before serving.

10 ripe peaches
¼ cup lemon juice
2½ cups confectioners' sugar
2 tablespoons peach brandy
10 egg whites
6 cups heavy cream
2 tablespoons granulated sugar

YIELD: 20 TO 24 SERVINGS.

Heidesand Cookies

Heidesand, meaning heather sand, cookies are so-called because of their slightly grainy texture, similar to the fine sand in which heather grows. This cookie batter needs to chill for at least 4 hours before baking.

½ pound (2 sticks) butter
1¼ cups sugar
1 vanilla bean
2½ cups unbleached white flour

Heat the butter in a heavy saucepan until amber colored. Remove from the heat and add the sugar, stirring until dissolved. Cool to room temperature.

Transfer the butter-sugar mixture to the bowl of an electric mixer and beat at high speed until fluffy. Squeeze in the essence of the vanilla bean, and add the flour. Beat at low speed until well blended.

Divide the dough in half, and shape into two 1½-inch-thick rolls. Place the rolls on a flat board or baking sheet, cover, and chill for at least 4 hours.

Preheat the oven to 350 degrees. Line 2 baking sheets with parchment paper.

Cut the rolls of dough into ¼-inch-thick slices, and place on the baking sheets, ½ inch apart.

Bake 18 minutes, or until the cookies feel firm when lightly touched. Remove from the oven and transfer to a countertop to cool completely. Stored in a covered tin, these cookies will last for up to 3 days.

YIELD: 60 COOKIES.

WEDDING RECEPTION
FOR FORTY

One of the most memorable moments in my life was the day Detlef and I were married, more than thirty-five years ago. After a brief ceremony, the wedding party gathered at my parents' home for the celebration. It makes me very happy to see that home weddings are experiencing a revival. There's nothing more satisfying than creating a feast that can be shared with family and friends on this most intimate of days.

Read through the menu and acquaint yourself with the various recipes. If you coordinate your shopping and prepare certain foods in ample time, this party could turn out to be one that you can pretty much manage on your own. I have put together a schedule that I hope will be helpful.

Starting three days before the wedding, bake the cakes, wrap them in plastic, and refrigerate. Cook the raspberry filling. This is also a good time to make the Apricot Sauce, and to prepare the Spinach Pockets. Store the pockets in the freezer until you're ready to bake them.

Two days ahead, make the Eggplant and Black Olive Dip. Bake the Chocolate Shortbread, and after cooling it sufficiently, store it in an airtight container. This is also when you should prepare the chicken pieces and refrigerate them. You can sauté them the day of the party.

The day before the wedding, bake the Pita Triangles and let them cool. Cover them in plastic and store at room temperature. Prepare the shrimp, and refrigerate until ready to serve. Bake the two frittatas and keep them refrigerated overnight, remembering to remove them in enough time so they are served at room temperature. Assemble the Snow Pea and Carrot Salad. Add the dressing just before serving time. Prepare the rice salad and, if necessary, add more dressing just before you serve. Bake the focaccia, cool, cover in plastic,

---

EGGPLANT AND BLACK OLIVE DIP WITH PITA TRIANGLES

SESAME CHICKEN WITH SPICY APRICOT SAUCE

SHRIMP WITH LEMON AND HERBS

SNOW PEA AND CARROT SALAD

GOAT CHEESE AND CHIVE FRITTATAS

SPINACH POCKETS

FOCACCIA WITH SAGE

RICE, TOMATO, AND BASIL SALAD

WHITE WEDDING CAKE WITH RASPBERRY MOUSSE FILLING AND FRESH FLOWERS

HEART-SHAPED CHOCOLATE SHORTBREAD

and store at room temperature. Most important, this is the time when you should assemble and frost the wedding cake and store it in the refrigerator. The flowers can be added at the last moment. Remember to read the instructions carefully. Don't be daunted, believe me, the recipes were designed to walk you through each procedure, step by step. It's deceptively easy.

Reserve the wedding day for sautéing the chicken and warming the Apricot Sauce. This is also when you can bake the Spinach Pockets and dress the salads. And finally, the cake. Adorn it with a magical cascade of beautiful summer flowers.

Eggplant and Black Olive Dip with Pita Triangles

One 1½-pound eggplant
1 teaspoon minced garlic
2 teaspoons olive oil
⅓ cup black olive purée
½ teaspoon freshly ground black pepper
12 large pita breads

Preheat the oven to 375 degrees.

Pierce the eggplant in several places with a fork. Bake it in a roasting pan until soft, about 30 minutes.

Scoop out the flesh and place it with the remaining ingredients except the pitas in the bowl of a food processor fitted with a steel blade. Pulse 4 times. The mixture should still be slightly coarse. Spoon into a 1½-quart serving bowl, and set aside.

Cut each pita into 8 wedges, pie fashion. Place the pieces on a baking sheet, and toast in the oven for 15 minutes, or until the edges are slightly browned.

Place the bowl of dip in the center of a large platter. Arrange the toasted pitas around the bowl. Serve at room temperature.

YIELD: 4 CUPS DIP, 96 PITA TRIANGLES.

Sesame Chicken with Spicy Apricot Sauce

This exotic recipe, halved, could serve 12 for lunch. Add a large green salad with a delicate vinaigrette, loaves of warmed French bread, sweet butter, and long, cool drinks.

Place all the sauce ingredients in a heavy saucepan over a low heat. Stirring occasionally, simmer until the apricot jelly has melted. Set aside.

Cut each chicken breast into 8 strips.

Combine the flour, sesame seeds, salt, and pepper in a large shallow pan, and dredge the chicken pieces in the mixture.

Cover the bottom of a large skillet with ½ inch peanut oil. Over medium heat, sauté the sesame-coated chicken pieces in batches for about 7 minutes, turning once, until browned and cooked throughout. Place the browned chicken in 2 large casseroles, and keep warm in a 200-degree oven for up to 30 minutes.

Just before serving, reheat the sauce and spoon a little over the chicken, placing the remainder in a sauceboat to pass separately. Garnish with parsley sprigs.

YIELD: 40 SERVINGS.

SAUCE

3 cups apricot jelly
1⅓ cups Balsamic vinegar
¼ cup soy sauce
1 teaspoon red pepper flakes

SESAME CHICKEN

15 pounds boneless, skinless chicken
    breasts
3 cups unbleached white flour
3 cups sesame seeds
3 tablespoons coarse salt
1 tablespoon freshly ground black
    pepper
Peanut oil

1 bunch parsley sprigs

Shrimp with Lemon and Herbs

10 pounds shrimp (28 to 30 count per
    pound), poached and shelled
6 cups finely chopped celery
3 cups finely chopped scallions
2 tablespoons grated lemon peel
3 seedless cucumbers
½ cup lemon juice
4 cups mayonnaise
1 teaspoon Tabasco
1 tablespoon coarse salt
1 cup finely chopped lemon balm or ¾
    cup finely chopped fresh mint
    combined with 1 teaspoon grated
    lemon peel
1 cup finely chopped mint
1 cup finely chopped oregano
Salad greens, enough to line a large
    bowl
Herb sprigs for garnish

Combine the cooked shrimp, celery, scallions, and grated lemon peel in a large mixing bowl. Slice 2 cucumbers into paper-thin rounds, and add to the bowl.

Whisk together the lemon juice, mayonnaise, Tabasco, and salt in a small bowl. Pour over the shrimp mixture and toss lightly. Add the fresh herbs, and toss again.

Spoon the shrimp salad into a bowl lined with salad greens. Garnish with the remaining cucumber, sliced thinly, and sprigs of herbs.

YIELD: 40 SERVINGS.

Snow Pea and Carrot Salad

7 pounds snow peas, julienned
7 pounds carrots, julienned
4 teaspoons grated lemon peel

DRESSING
¾ cup lemon juice
2 cups extra-virgin olive oil
⅓ cup Dijon mustard
1½ tablespoons coarse salt
1 teaspoon Tabasco

Place the snow peas, carrots, and lemon peel in a large serving bowl.

Combine the dressing ingredients in a quart container with a screw-top lid. Shake vigorously, and pour over the vegetables. Toss to blend.

YIELD: 40 SERVINGS.

Goat Cheese and Chive Frittatas

A creamy, savory dish that is superb as a late-night supper, served with a crisp chicory salad dressed with a light vinaigrette.

Preheat the oven to 350 degrees. Butter two 12 x 17 x 1-inch baking sheets.

Place ½ cup of flour, 1½ teaspoons baking powder, 17 eggs, and ½ pound of butter in the large bowl of a food processor fitted with a steel blade. Pulse 6 times. Transfer the mixture to a larger mixing bowl.

Add 1¼ cups of the grated Gruyère, 1 cup of the crumbled Boucheron, 2 cups of cottage cheese, ½ teaspoon of salt, 1 teaspoon of pepper and ½ cup of chopped chives, and mix thoroughly. Pour into the first prepared baking sheet. Repeat the above procedure with the remaining ingredients and pour into the second baking sheet.

Bake the frittatas for 25 minutes, or until the custard is set and lightly browned. Remove from the oven, and cut each frittata into 24 small pieces. Pile the pieces on a large serving platter, and serve warm.

YIELD: 2 FRITTATAS, 48 SMALL PIECES.

1 cup unbleached white flour
3 teaspoons baking powder
34 large eggs
1 pound (4 sticks) butter, melted
2½ cups (10 ounces) grated Gruyère cheese
2 cups (10 ounces) crumbled Boucheron cheese
4 cups cottage cheese
1 teaspoon coarse salt
2 teaspoons freshly ground black pepper
1 cup finely chopped chives or scallions
½ cup capers

Spinach Pockets

A flaky, buttery treasure chest filled with mellow spinach in a savory, creamy base.

2 tablespoons olive oil
2½ cups finely chopped onions
Four 10-ounce packages frozen chopped
   spinach, defrosted
3 eggs
1 cup crumbled feta cheese
½ cup grated Parmesan cheese
¾ teaspoon coarse salt
1 teaspoon freshly ground black pepper
1¼ cups chopped parsley
Two 1-pound packages phyllo pastry,
   12 x 17 inches in size
¾ pound (3 sticks) butter, melted

Heat the olive oil in a medium sauté pan. Add the onions, and sauté until they are transparent. Remove from the heat.

Press all the water out of the defrosted spinach and add to the onions, along with the eggs, feta, Parmesan, salt, pepper, and parsley. Mix thoroughly and chill for 1 hour.

Follow the directions on the phyllo dough package by carefully layering 3 sheets of phyllo, brushing each layer with melted butter.

Preheat the oven to 400 degrees.

Cut the phyllo into 6 even squares. Place 1 rounded teaspoon of spinach filling on top of each square. Fold down into a triangle, as you would a flag. Brush each finished triangle with butter, and place on a buttered baking sheet. Repeat this process until all the filling is used.

Bake 12 to 15 minutes, or until browned and puffy.

YIELD: 80 POCKETS.

Focaccia with Sage

A delicious, flat herbed bread that's simple to make. For a variation, substitute fresh thyme leaves for the sage.

2 tablespoons active dry yeast
5 cups warm water
14 cups unbleached white flour
¾ cup olive oil
4 tablespoons coarse salt
1 cup chopped fresh sage

Combine the yeast with 5 cups of warm water in a large mixing bowl. Let stand for 5 minutes until the yeast is dissolved.

Add 13 cups of flour, ½ cup of olive oil, and 1 tablespoon of salt. Using your hands, mix the ingredients well. Turn the dough out onto a lightly floured countertop, and, using the remaining flour, knead for about 10 minutes, until the dough is smooth and elastic.

Transfer the dough to a clean bowl, and let rest in a warm place about 1½ hours, or until doubled in bulk.

Preheat the oven to 400 degrees.

Brush two 12 x 17 x 1-inch baking sheets with some of the remaining olive oil. Divide the dough in half. Press the dough to fit the shape of each pan, brush with the remaining olive oil, and sprinkle with the remaining salt and sage.

Let rise 15 minutes, then bake 20 minutes, or until light brown. Cut the bread into 2½ x 1½-inch pieces.

YIELD: 2 LARGE FLAT BREADS, SERVING 40.

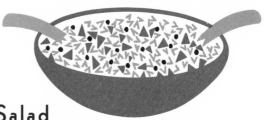

Rice, Tomato, and Basil Salad

Combine the dressing ingredients in a screw-top jar, and shake vigorously until the salt and sugar are dissolved. Set aside.

Bring the rice and 5 quarts of water to a boil, cover, and simmer for 12 minutes, or until the rice is just tender.

Transfer the cooked rice to a large serving bowl, add the tomatoes and the dressing, and mix well. Keep the salad for up to 3 hours at room temperature, until ready to serve. Just before serving, fold in the basil leaves.

NOTE: Covered and refrigerated, leftovers will last for 1 more day.

YIELD: 40 SERVINGS.

DRESSING

2 cups rice vinegar
½ cup sugar
2 tablespoons coarse salt
⅔ cup olive oil
2 teaspoons freshly ground black
   pepper

7½ cups white rice
8 cups (8 medium) tomatoes, cut into
   ½-inch cubes
8 cups coarsely chopped, loosely packed
   basil leaves (2 bunches)

White Wedding Cake with Raspberry Mousse Filling and Fresh Flowers

Read this entire recipe over carefully before you proceed. You will see that the cake needs to be made in 3 batches. In order to simplify this recipe, I have listed the ingredients for 1 batch of cake batter, which will make 1 large or 2 small tiers. I have done it this way because when dealing with ingredients such as separated eggs and baking soda, it is very important that the measurements be accurate. One batch of filling and frosting ingredients, as listed below, is enough to cover all 4 tiers, but you will need to make 3 batches of cake batter.

CAKE BATTER (1 BATCH)

1 pound butter, softened
3 cups sugar
8 eggs, separated, at room temperature
2 teaspoons vanilla extract
6 cups unbleached white flour
2 tablespoons baking powder
1 teaspoon baking soda
2 cups milk

Butter the bottom and sides of one 12-inch, one 10-inch, one 8-inch, and one 6-inch round cake pan, all 2½ inches deep. Line the bottom of each pan with parchment paper, and butter the paper.

Preheat the oven to 325 degrees.

One batch of cake batter makes the 12-inch layer. In the bowl of an electric mixer, cream the butter and sugar until light. Add the egg yolks, vanilla, and 2 cups of flour. Beat at low speed to mix well. Add 2 more cups of flour, the baking powder, baking soda, and milk. Combine the mixture at low speed before adding the remaining 2 cups of flour and mixing to blend.

Transfer the batter to a larger mixing bowl.

In a clean bowl, whip the egg whites until soft peaks hold. Gently fold the egg whites into the cake batter. Spoon the batter into the prepared 12-inch cake pan.

Bake 1 hour 40 minutes, or until a toothpick inserted in the center comes out clean.

While the 12-inch layer is baking, make another batch of cake batter. Spoon all but 2 cups into the prepared 10-inch cake pan. Bake 1 hour 20 minutes, or until a toothpick inserted in the center comes out clean. If you can whip up the second batch of batter in 20 minutes, you can synchronize the baking of both cakes so that they finish at the same time.

Make the third batch of cake batter. Add this to the remaining 2 cups of batter from the second batch. Divide it between the prepared 8-inch and 6-inch cake pans.

Bake the 8-inch cake for 1 hour 10 minutes, and the 6-inch cake for 1 hour, or until done.

Cool the cakes in their pans. Wrap the cooled cakes and pans in plastic wrap and store in the refrigerator for up to 2 days.

To make the filling, drain the thawed raspberries, catching the juice in a small heavy saucepan. Set the raspberries aside.

Whisk the potato starch and sugar into the raspberry juice and, stirring constantly, bring the mixture to a boil. Once thickened, remove from the heat.

Fold the raspberries and the Framboise into the thickened mixture, and chill for up to 2 days.

To moisten the cakes, bring 2½ cups of water and ¾ cup sugar to a boil, stirring constantly. Cool. Add the Framboise, and chill for up to 2 days.

Assemble the cake on the morning of the wedding. Cut all the cakes in half horizontally. Moisten by sprinkling each layer with some of the Framboise syrup.

Whip 3 cups of heavy cream until firm. Fold into the raspberry mixture. Smooth the bottom half of each cake with some of the raspberry filling, and place the tops back on each cake.

To make the frosting, combine all the ingredients in the large bowl of an electric mixer. Beat at a high speed until very fluffy (depending on the size of your mixer you may need to do this in 2 batches).

Frost the tops and sides of all 4 cakes.

Set the 12-inch cake onto a 14-inch cake plate. Place the 10-inch cake on top of the 12-inch cake, making sure to center it properly. Place the 8-inch on the 10-inch, and the 6-inch on the 8-inch, centering each one. Use the frosting to repair any flaws and to fill in the gaps where the layers meet.

Insert wooden skewers, evenly spaced, down through the cakes to hold them in place.

Spoon the remaining frosting into a pastry bag fitted with a star tip. Decorate the cake by making star flowers, creating a cascading effect over the cake.

Place a small bouquet of fresh flowers on top of the cake, pushing them slightly into the 6-inch cake.

Garnish the cake with more flowers and lemon leaves. Store the cake in the refrigerator until ready to serve.

To cut the cake, remove the top layer and set it on a dinner

FILLING

Four 10-ounce packages frozen
    raspberries in light syrup, thawed
3 tablespoons potato starch
¾ cup sugar
2 tablespoons Framboise liqueur
3 cups heavy cream

FRAMBOISE SYRUP

2½ cups water
¾ cup sugar
¼ cup Framboise liqueur

FROSTING

6 pounds confectioners' sugar
14 egg whites
20 tablespoons (2½ sticks) butter,
    softened
2 teaspoons vanilla extract
1 teaspoon almond extract

GARNISH AND ASSEMBLY

Fresh flowers and lemon leaves
Four 8-inch wooden skewers

(continued)

plate. This is usually not served. Cut the second layer into wedges, and when they have all gone do the same with the third and then the fourth layer.

YIELD: 50 SERVINGS.

Heart-Shaped Chocolate Shortbread

If you prefer golden shortbread, merely substitute equal portions of flour for the cocoa.

4 cups unbleached white flour
1½ cups Swiss cocoa
2½ cups confectioners' sugar
2 teaspoons vanilla extract
1 pound 2 ounces (4½ sticks) cold
    butter, cut into small pieces

Place half of all the ingredients in the bowl of a food processor fitted with a steel blade. Process until the mixture forms a ball. Turn the mixture out onto a lightly floured countertop. Knead a few times, wrap in plastic, and chill for 30 minutes. Repeat the process with the remaining ingredients.

Preheat the oven to 325 degrees.

Roll out 1 ball at a time, ¼ inch thick. Using a heart-shaped cookie cutter, cut as many cookies as possible. Place the cookies on an ungreased baking sheet.

Repeat the rolling and cookie-cutting process until all the dough has been used.

Bake the cookies 15 to 20 minutes, or until the shortbread feels firm when lightly touched.

Remove from the oven and cool. Store the cooled cookies in an airtight container for up to 3 days.

YIELD: 60 COOKIES.

FOURTH OF JULY CELEBRATION
FOR SIXTEEN

By the first week of July, our garden behind Loaves and Fishes is chock full of delicious treats. Fresh basil, dill, rosemary, and thyme fill the air with a swirling bouquet of inspirational aromas. Snap peas, sweet and crunchy, hang from their vines just waiting to be picked. Young, red tomatoes, warmed by the sun, drop into your hands. Onions, celery, and early yellow and red bell peppers not only add color to the garden, but emit a strong, distinctive scent all their own. With this great wealth of goodies at our fingertips, we created the following festive menu for a large July Fourth celebration, and modified it slightly to fit a smaller gathering. If you feel venturesome, the recipes can all be doubled quite easily.

The Dill Bread can be made a week before the party and kept wrapped in the freezer until the day before. Make sure it's thoroughly defrosted; it's best when slightly warmed or served at room temperature.

The day before the party is a perfect time to poach, marinate, and refrigerate the tuna. It'll give the tuna time to set and harden slightly, making it a more substantial and meatier addition to your salad.

I'd suggest you bake the cherry pie the day before, and after letting it cool, cover the pie with plastic wrap and leave it at room temperature.

The day of the party, prepare the potato salad. It's best when made no longer than 3 hours before serving, and should be served at room temperature.

The fillets need to marinate 2 hours before baking. After cooking, allow the meat to rest for 20 minutes before slicing to serve.

When it's time to assemble the tomatoes and onions, slice them about ½-inch thick—medium-sized tomatoes yield

---

FILLET OF BEEF IN
HONEY-ROSEMARY MARINADE

FRESH TUNA SALAD

NEW POTATOES IN
BASIL CREAM

SUGAR SNAP PEAS WITH
SESAME SEED DRESSING

SLICED TOMATO AND
RED ONION

DILL BREAD

BLACK CHERRY PIE

VANILLA ICE CREAM

about 4 thick slices—and figure on 2 slices of tomato and 1 slice of onion per person. To enjoy tomatoes at their peak, always serve them at room temperature.

Read through the menu carefully before starting. You'll see that it's filled with a variety of taste sensations and an abundance of additional menu suggestions. You may also notice a predominance of red and white foods. It was intentional, we were hoping that Mother Nature would do her part for the celebration by contributing a blue sky.

Fillet of Beef in Honey-Rosemary Marinade

When cut into strips, leftover fillet can be incorporated into a fabulous salad. Add your favorite greens, some cut-up tomatoes, onions, toasted sesame seeds, marinated artichoke hearts—whatever tickles your palate. Sprinkle it with a snappy, mustardy vinaigrette, and presto—you've created another meal!

Two 6- to 7-pound fillets of beef, trimmed
½ cup olive oil
2 teaspoons minced garlic
¾ cup soy sauce
½ cup honey
¼ cup curry powder
2 tablespoons fresh rosemary leaves
8 sprigs fresh rosemary

Place the beef in a roasting pan large enough so the fillets don't touch.

Place the remaining ingredients, except the fresh rosemary sprigs, in a screw-top jar. Shake vigorously and pour the mixture over the meat. Marinate 2 hours at room temperature.

Preheat the oven to 500 degrees.

Roast the fillets, uncovered, for 17 minutes. Remove from the oven, cover with foil, and let stand on a countertop close to the oven for 20 minutes.

To serve, carve the meat into ¼-inch-thick slices, on a slight diagonal. Arrange on a serving platter and drizzle with the pan juices. Garnish with sprigs of fresh rosemary.

YIELD: 16 SERVINGS.

Fresh Tuna Salad

Add some steamed green beans, poached baby potatoes, hard-boiled eggs, maybe an avocado, sliced tomatoes, and julienned endive, and you have the most superb lunch. All you need is a loaf of black bread and a bottle of chilled white wine.

Pour the wine and 4 cups of cold water into a large skillet. Add the onion, bay leaf, and 1½ teaspoons of salt, and bring to a boil. Reduce the heat, and simmer, covered, for 5 minutes.

Making sure not to crowd the skillet, poach the tuna, 3 or 4 slices at a time, for about 10 minutes, or until just done. Continue poaching until all the tuna is cooked. Transfer the fish to a glass or earthenware casserole, placing the slices in a single layer. Pour the two vinegars over the fish, cover, and chill for 6 hours, or overnight.

To make the salad, break the tuna into bite-size pieces, and place in a serving bowl. Add the rest of the ingredients except the dill sprigs. Mix gently with your hands until well blended, taking care not to overmix; the salad should be chunky, not mushy.

Garnish with fresh dill sprigs.

2 cups dry white wine
I small onion, cut in half
I bay leaf
1½ teaspoons coarse salt
6 pounds fresh tuna, sliced I inch thick
⅓ cup distilled white vinegar
½ cup white wine vinegar
2 cups finely chopped celery
3 cups finely chopped red onions
I tablespoon freshly ground black
    pepper
½ cup drained capers
2 cups chopped fresh dill
3 cups mayonnaise
6 sprigs dill

YIELD: 16 SERVINGS.

New Potatoes in Basil Cream

6 pounds small new potatoes
¾ cup hot chicken stock (page 8)

BASIL CREAM

4 cups loosely packed fresh basil leaves
1 teaspoon minced garlic
2 tablespoons lemon juice
2 teaspoons freshly ground black
  pepper
1 tablespoon coarse salt
1 tablespoon honey mustard
1 cup heavy cream
1 cup mayonnaise

Place the potatoes in a large pot. Cover with cold water and bring to a boil. Reduce the heat, and simmer, uncovered, until just tender, about 12 to 15 minutes. Drain.

Cut the warm potatoes into bite-size pieces, and place in a mixing bowl. Pour the hot chicken stock over the potatoes.

To make the dressing, place the basil leaves and garlic in the bowl of a food processor fitted with a steel blade. Process until smooth. Add the lemon juice, pepper, salt, mustard, and cream. Process 5 seconds. Add the mayonnaise, and pulse a few times just to blend. Pour the basil cream over the potatoes, using your hands to mix well. Spoon the salad into a large bowl, and serve at room temperature.

YIELD: 16 SERVINGS.

Sugar Snap Peas with Sesame Seed Dressing

Hot or cold, this dish goes well with broiled and grilled meats. You can substitute snow peas, and if you want a milder dish, omit the red pepper flakes.

4 pounds sugar snap or snow peas
⅓ cup sesame seeds
½ cup sesame oil
2 teaspoons red pepper flakes
2 teaspoons coarse salt

Blanch the peas in a large quantity of boiling water just until they turn bright green, about 1 minute. Drain and plunge the peas into very cold water to stop the cooking process. Drain again. Transfer the peas to a mixing bowl.

Place the sesame seeds in a large skillet over medium heat. Tossing lightly, toast until golden brown, and add to the sugar snap peas.

In the same skillet, heat the sesame oil until smoking hot. Remove from the heat, and add the red pepper flakes. Let stand for 5 minutes. Pour the oil over the peas, add the salt, and toss to blend. Transfer the peas to a deep bowl or platter, and serve hot.

YIELD: 16 SERVINGS.

Dill Bread

*In the winter you can substitute 2 tablespoons of dill seed for the
fresh dill in this aromatic bread.*

Heat the safflower oil in a skillet. Add the onions, and sauté
until soft. Remove from heat.

Pour the warm water into a large mixing bowl. Add the
yeast and sugar. Let stand for 5 minutes. Stir in the cottage
cheese, dill, salt, eggs, and onions.

Add 2½ cups of flour and the baking soda. Mix until well
blended, about 5 minutes. Add the remaining flour, and mix
about 3 minutes more. The dough should be very soft.

Cover the bowl with a kitchen towel, and let rise in a warm
place for 1 hour.

Spoon the dough into two 5 x 9-inch loaf pans. Cover with
the towel and let rise for 40 minutes, or until doubled in
bulk.

Preheat the oven to 350 degrees.

Bake 40 minutes, or until the loaves sound hollow when
tapped on top. Remove from the oven, cool 10 minutes, then
remove from the pans.

½ cup safflower oil
1½ cups finely chopped onions
1⅓ cups warm water
2 tablespoons active dry yeast
2 teaspoons sugar
2 cups small-curd cottage cheese
1 cup finely chopped fresh dill
1½ tablespoons coarse salt
2 eggs
5 cups unbleached white flour
2 teaspoons baking soda

YIELD: 2 LOAVES, 10 SLICES EACH.

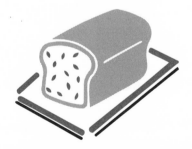

Black Cherry Pie

PASTRY

7 cups unbleached white flour
¼ cup sugar
1 pound (4 sticks) cold butter, cut into
    small pieces
½ teaspoon salt
4 egg yolks

FILLING

4 pounds pitted black cherries
¾ cup unbleached white flour
2 cups sugar
3 tablespoons lemon juice
1 teaspoon ground cinnamon

Vanilla Ice Cream (page 58) (optional)

Place all the pastry ingredients in the bowl of an electric mixer. Mix at low speed just to blend. Turn the dough out onto a flour-dusted countertop and gather it into a ball. Wrap in wax paper and chill for 30 minutes.

Preheat the oven to 425 degrees.

Cut the dough in half. Roll one half into a 14 x 19-inch rectangle. Fit this dough into a 12 x 17-inch baking sheet.

In a large bowl, thoroughly mix together the filling ingredients. Spread evenly over the pastry crust.

Roll out the remaining dough into a 12 x 17-inch rectangle. Roll it onto a rolling pin, and carefully unroll it over the cherry filling. Using a fork, seal the edges. Cut slits in the top of the crust at 3-inch intervals. Bake 50 minutes.

Remove from the oven, and cool and store at room temperature.

Serve from the pan, either warm or at room temperature, with Vanilla Ice Cream, if desired.

YIELD: 16 SERVINGS.

SUMMER DINNER
FOR TWELVE

This is one of my favorite menus. It was conceived out of necessity during a patch of turbulent summer weather. What was planned as a buffet dinner on a patio turned into a stately dinner for twelve, served around a beautifully set dining-room table. With tropical winds wafting in through the opened windows—rain pounding against the shingled roof —candlelight sputtering on the tables, flowers in abundance, and soft music playing under the occasional crash of thunder, everyone seemed supremely happy as they chatted over this elegant meal.

The meal begins with the thinnest slices of fresh salmon, served with a Honey-Mustard Sauce and sprinkled with plump and pungent capers. For the ultimate in freshness, be sure to inform your fishmonger that you plan to serve the salmon raw.

Cornish Hens crisped with an Apricot Glaze are ideally easy to prepare. If you wish, stuff the birds with the cooked rice before baking, then serve them on a bed of the remaining reheated wild rice. The sautéed beans can be served on the same plate.

And for the grand finale, Cocoa Cups filled with Vanilla Ice Cream and crowned with luscious strawberries.

Here are a few suggestions to help you create this menu with seamless precision and a minimum of fuss.

Make the Honey-Mustard Sauce, Apricot Glaze, and Cocoa Cups the day before the party.

The beans can be blanched and the rice cooked a few hours ahead. The salmon should be sliced at the last minute. Place 2 slices on each plate.

The Cornish Hens take only an hour to bake and a few minutes to prepare. The dessert can be assembled just before serving.

> SALMON WITH
> HONEY-MUSTARD SAUCE
>
> CORNISH HENS WITH
> APRICOT GLAZE
>
> GREEN AND
> YELLOW BEAN SAUTÉ
>
> WILD RICE
>
> ---
>
> COCOA CUPS WITH ICE
> CREAM
> AND STRAWBERRIES

Salmon with Honey-Mustard Sauce

½ cup honey
I cup Dijon mustard
½ teaspoon coarse salt
I teaspoon freshly ground black pepper
I cup finely chopped fresh dill
One 3½-pound, very fresh salmon fillet
6 lemons
12 sprigs fresh dill
¼ cup olive oil
¼ cup capers

Warm the honey in a small saucepan. Remove from the heat, and add the mustard, salt, pepper, and chopped dill. Stir to mix well and set aside.

Place the salmon, skin side down, on a cutting board. Cut the fish on the diagonal into 24 very thin slices. Chill until ready to use.

To make the lemons into cups, halve them through the middle. Extract and save the juice, remove the remaining pulp, and cut a thin slice off the bottom of each lemon half so it will stand on the plate. Divide the honey-mustard sauce among the hollowed-out lemon halves.

Arrange 1 dill sprig, 2 slices of salmon, and 1 sauce-filled lemon cup on each first-course plate. Sprinkle 1 teaspoon of lemon juice, olive oil, and capers over the salmon slices, and serve.

YIELD: 12 SERVINGS.

Cornish Hens with Apricot Glaze

APRICOT GLAZE

¾ cup (1¼ pounds) dried apricots, or
    1½ cups (1 pound) fresh, if
    available
I cup white wine
½ cup apricot jelly
I teaspoon minced garlic
I tablespoon minced fresh gingerroot
I teaspoon chili powder
2 tablespoons Dijon mustard
1½ teaspoons coarse salt
I teaspoon freshly ground black pepper

Twelve I-pound Cornish hens
Olive oil

To make the glaze, combine all the ingredients in a heavy saucepan. Simmer 10 minutes. Transfer to a food processor fitted with a steel blade, and purée until smooth. Set aside.

Preheat the oven to 375 degrees.

Rub the hens with the olive oil, and place on a baking sheet. Bake for a total of 1 hour, glazing the birds twice during the last 20 minutes.

To serve, place 1 hen on each dinner plate. Reheat the remaining glaze in a small saucepan, pour into a sauceboat, and pass separately.

YIELD: 12 SERVINGS.

Green and Yellow Bean Sauté

Buttery beans flavored with mellow and fragrant tarragon leaves.

Fill a large pot half full of water. Bring to a boil. Add the beans, and cook until the green beans turn a bright green, about 30 seconds after the water returns to a boil. Drain and cool the beans quickly by running cold water over them. Drain well, and dry in a kitchen towel.

In a large sauté pan, heat the oil and butter until the butter starts to bubble. Add the beans. Sauté over medium heat for about 5 minutes, until the beans are heated through. Add the tarragon, salt, and pepper; serve immediately.

1½ pounds green beans, trimmed
1½ pounds yellow beans, trimmed
¼ cup olive oil
6 tablespoons butter
¼ cup loosely packed fresh tarragon
　leaves
1 tablespoon coarse salt
2 teaspoons freshly ground black
　pepper

YIELD: 12 SERVINGS.

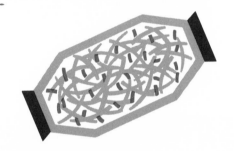

Wild Rice

Heat the butter in a large saucepan until it starts to bubble. Add the onions, and sauté over low heat for 5 minutes. Add the wild rice, chicken stock, salt, and pepper. Bring to a boil, cover, and simmer for 35 minutes, or until the rice is al dente. Remove from the heat, fold in the scallions and serve hot.

4 tablespoons butter
2 cups finely chopped onions
2¼ cups wild rice
5½ cups chicken stock (page 8)
2 teaspoons coarse salt
1 teaspoon freshly ground black pepper
2 cups chopped scallion greens

YIELD: 12 SERVINGS.

Cocoa Cups with Ice Cream and Strawberries

This dessert is requested over and over again. I suggest that you make these often, starting with the Cocoa Cups and allowing your own personal taste and ingenuity to guide you in choosing other scrumptious fillings: peach yogurt topped with chunks of fresh peaches and touched with only a trickle of peach brandy, chocolate ice cream with grated chocolate and whipped cream, coffee ice cream bathed in hot chocolate and decorated with raspberries.

4 egg whites
12 tablespoons (1½ sticks) butter, softened
½ cup sugar
½ cup Dutch cocoa
½ cup unbleached white flour
1 teaspoon ground cinnamon
3 pints Vanilla Ice Cream (page 58)
3 pints fresh strawberries, hulled

Preheat the oven to 375 degrees. Butter three 18 x 12 x 1-inch baking sheets.

Beat the egg whites in the bowl of an electric mixer until soft peaks hold. Transfer to another bowl.

Using the same electric mixer bowl, cream the butter and sugar until light. Add the cocoa, flour, and cinnamon, and mix to blend well. Using a rubber spatula, fold the egg whites into the cocoa batter.

Make 12 cocoa balls by dropping 4 heaping tablespoonsful of batter on each prepared baking sheet. Spread each ball into a 5½-inch circle. Bake about 7 to 8 minutes, until firm. Using a metal spatula, lift each cocoa round off the baking sheet and place over the bottom of an inverted drinking glass. Let the cocoa cups cool in place for 1 hour, then carefully remove and turn right-side up. Just before serving, fill each cup with ice cream and strawberries.

YIELD: 12 SERVINGS.

COOL SUMMER LUNCH
FOR EIGHT

This is a perfect lunch to serve under a shady tree, picnic-style, with a pretty patchwork quilt as a tablecloth.

The soup and the dessert are best made one day in advance.

The Lemon-Basil Chicken Salad can be prepared the night before and stored in the refrigerator.

The corn sticks should be baked no more than 3 hours ahead.

CHILLED CARROT SOUP

LEMON-BASIL CHICKEN
SALAD

CORN STICKS

FROZEN PEACH YOGURT
WITH POACHED PEACHES

Chilled Carrot Soup

Sweet fresh carrots combined with onions, ginger, and curry make this soup equally delicious hot or cold.

Heat the olive oil in a large heavy saucepan. Sauté the onions over low heat for about 10 minutes. Add the garlic, ginger, carrots, curry powder, pepper, and salt. Stir to mix. Add the chicken stock, bring to a boil, and simmer, covered, for 30 minutes.

Remove from the heat and cool to room temperature before puréeing the soup in batches until smooth.

Chill for at least 6 hours. Garnish with fresh chives.

¼ cup olive oil
2 cups chopped onions
2 teaspoons minced garlic
2 tablespoons minced fresh gingerroot
2 pounds carrots, peeled and chopped
2 teaspoons curry powder
½ teaspoon freshly ground black
   pepper
2 teaspoons coarse salt
10 cups chicken stock
¼ cup chopped fresh chives

YIELD: 8 SERVINGS.

Lemon-Basil Chicken Salad

If basil is not available, tarragon is a good substitute.

5 pounds chicken breasts, skinned and boned

I cup thinly sliced red onions, cut in half moons

½ cup green or red seedless grapes, cut in half

2 cups snow peas, or sugar snap peas, cut in half

I cup chopped fresh basil leaves

DRESSING

3½ cups mayonnaise

⅓ cup lemon juice

2 tablespoons grated lemon peel

1½ teaspoons coarse salt

¼ teaspoon freshly ground black pepper

2 tablespoons white wine

3 sprigs fresh basil

In a medium saucepan three-quarters full of boiling water, poach the chicken breasts for 10 minutes, or until done. Remove the cooked chicken from the liquid, and let cool until comfortable enough to handle. Discard the water.

Cut the cooked chicken into 1-inch cubes, and place in a large mixing bowl. Add the red onions, grapes, snow peas, and basil leaves.

Combine the dressing ingredients, and stir to blend. Pour over the chicken salad. Mix gently but thoroughly with your hands. Transfer to a serving platter and garnish with sprigs of fresh basil.

YIELD: 8 TO 10 SERVINGS.

Corn Sticks

Line a pretty basket with a colorful napkin and serve these delicious golden treats hot out of the oven.

Preheat the oven to 375 degrees. Butter a baking sheet.

Place the flour, cornmeal, baking powder, salt, and butter in the bowl of a food processor fitted with a steel blade. Pulse 10 times, to break up the butter. Add the cheddar cheese and pulse once, then add the eggs and pulse once. Finally, add the milk and pulse 4 times.

Turn the dough out onto a flour-dusted countertop. Roll into a 16 x 3-inch strip. Cut into 1-inch sticks, and place on the prepared baking sheet.

Bake 30 to 35 minutes, or until golden. Serve hot.

1½ cups unbleached white flour
1 cup coarse yellow cornmeal
1 teaspoon baking powder
¼ teaspoon coarse salt
8 tablespoons (1 stick) cold butter, cut into 8 pieces
¾ cup (¼ pound) grated cheddar cheese
2 eggs
¾ cup milk

YIELD: 16 CORN STICKS.

Frozen Peach Yogurt with Poached Peaches

Peel, pit, and coarsely chop 4 of the peaches. Place in the bowl of a food processor fitted with a steel blade, along with ¼ cup of the crystallized ginger, the honey, confectioners' sugar, and lemon juice. Pulse 5 or 6 times; the mixture should be a bit chunky. Fold in the yogurt, and freeze in an ice cream maker following the manufacturer's instructions.

In a saucepan, bring the remaining ginger, white wine, water, and sugar to a boil. Reduce the heat to a simmer.

Peel, pit, and quarter the remaining peaches. Cook them in the sugar syrup for about 10 minutes. Remove from the heat, transfer the peaches and syrup to a glass or earthenware bowl, and chill, uncovered, for 6 hours.

To serve, divide the peaches among 8 dessert plates. Top with the frozen peach yogurt, and garnish with a fresh mint sprig.

8 ripe peaches
½ cup minced crystallized ginger
½ cup honey
½ cup confectioners' sugar
1 tablespoon lemon juice
4 cups plain yogurt
¾ cup dry white wine
¾ cup water
¾ cup granulated sugar
8 fresh mint sprigs

YIELD: 8 SERVINGS.

COCKTAIL PARTY ON THE LAWN
FOR FORTY

SUN-DRIED TOMATO BAKED
ON FRENCH BREAD

COCONUT SHRIMP WITH
LIME SAUCE

ONION TART

LOBSTER STRUDELS

MEXICAN EGGS

FALAFEL WITH
CUCUMBER RAITA

BEEF AND SCALLION ROLLS

Every year Sybille and I travel with our families, rounding up as many new and challenging recipes as we can find. I'm so thankful that Detlef is such a willing guinea pig. He loves to order any dish he thinks might be unusual and tasty, and invariably, with some minor adjustments, it ends up in our growing repertoire of recipes.

Sybille's husband, Michael, also a cook and gourmet, shares our daughter's enthusiasm for provocative cuisine. When we were asked recently to cater a cocktail party for forty, Sybille and I pooled our resources and came up with what seems like an international feast. With a little adaptation here and there, we were able to format it so you can prepare the same menu with only a minimum of fuss.

The Lobster Strudels can be made up to 4 weeks ahead of time, wrapped in foil, and frozen. They can be baked when ready to serve. The Lime Sauce and Cucumber Raita can be made 2 days ahead and refrigerated. This is also a good time to begin making the falafels by soaking the chick-peas overnight. The next day you can assemble and shape the falafel mixture and refrigerate.

The day before the cocktail party, make the sun-dried tomato mixture and refrigerate. The egg cups and salsalike filling can be made then, too, and stored in the refrigerator. The 24 hard-boiled egg yolks will last 4 days when refrigerated. Crumble them over tomorrow's salad, saving a few to enrich the vinaigrette.

The day of the party, fry the falafels. You can reheat them just before serving. Make the Beef and Scallion Rolls, and bake them just before serving. The Mexican Egg filling can be cooked and just before serving can be stuffed into the egg cups.

The Coconut Shrimp should be cooked no more than 3 hours before serving.

If you've never dared to serve cocktails for forty on your own before, this would be an excellent menu with which to start. Make sure there are plenty of mixers and ice on hand. Set the array of gorgeous foods on a long buffet table, get yourself a long, cool drink, and treat yourself as one of your guests.

Sun-Dried Tomato Baked on French Bread

Place all the ingredients except the bread in the bowl of a food processor fitted with a steel blade. Process until finely chopped.

Preheat the oven to 400 degrees.

Slice each loaf of bread into 20 even slices, ¾-inch thick. Spread a little sun-dried tomato mixture on each piece of bread. Arrange the slices on a baking sheet and bake until the edges of the bread are light brown, about 10 to 12 minutes.

Serve warm.

2 teaspoons minced garlic
4 cups loosely packed fresh basil leaves
1½ cups coarsely chopped sun-dried
    tomatoes
6 tablespoons olive oil
1 teaspoon coarse salt
1 teaspoon freshly ground black pepper
3 loaves French bread, 15 inches long

YIELD: 60 CROSTINI.

Coconut Shrimp with Lime Sauce

LIME SAUCE

1 cup chopped fresh chives or scallion
   greens

1½ teaspoons grated lime peel

⅓ cup lime juice

2 cups mayonnaise

¾ teaspoon coarse salt

¾ teaspoon freshly ground black
   pepper

COCONUT SHRIMP

4 pounds shrimp (21 to 25 count per
   pound), peeled and deveined

3 egg whites, beaten with a fork

1 cup unsweetened coconut

1 cup unbleached white flour

2 teaspoons hot red pepper flakes

2 teaspoons ground cumin

2 teaspoons coarse salt

Peanut oil

Place the chives, grated lime peel, and lime juice in the bowl of a food processor fitted with a steel blade. Process for 1 minute. Add the mayonnaise, salt, and pepper. Process 1 minute more. Transfer the sauce to a covered container. Chill for 6 hours or up to 2 days.

Shortly before serving time, place the shrimp in a bowl. Pour the egg whites over them, and toss to coat.

In another small bowl, combine the coconut, flour, red pepper flakes, cumin, and salt. Add this dry mixture to the shrimp. Mix thoroughly to coat all the shrimp well.

Pour 1 inch of peanut oil into a large sauté pan. Heat until very hot, but not smoking. Cook the shrimp in 4 batches in the hot oil, for about 1 minute on each side.

Transfer the warm shrimp to a serving platter, and serve with the cold dipping sauce on the side.

YIELD: 40 SERVINGS.

Onion Tart

Custardy, savory, and satisfying; this is such an easy tart to make, and one that perfectly rounds out a buffet.

To make the pastry, place the flour, butter, and margarine in the bowl of a food processor fitted with a steel blade. Pulse 6 times, to blend the butter and margarine. Add the salt and cold water. Pulse 6 times. Turn the dough out onto a lightly floured countertop. Gather into a ball, wrap in wax paper, and refrigerate for 30 minutes.

Preheat the oven to 375 degrees.

Roll out the pastry to fit a 12 x 17 x 1-inch baking sheet. Trim the edges. Line the pastry shell with foil and weight with dried beans. Bake the shell for 15 minutes. Remove the beans and foil, and bake 10 minutes more.

To make the filling, heat the butter in a large sauté pan, add the onions, and sauté over low heat for about 15 minutes, until soft and transparent. Spread the onions evenly over the pastry shell. Sprinkle with the grated Gruyère. Combine the remaining ingredients in a bowl, and pour into the tart.

Bake for 35 minutes, or until the custard is set and the top is golden. Cut the tart into eighty-four 1 x 2-inch pieces, pile high on a platter, and serve warm.

YIELD: 84 PIECES.

PASTRY

3 cups unbleached white flour
¼ pound (1 stick) cold butter, cut into 8 pieces
¼ pound (1 stick) cold margarine, cut into 8 pieces
1 teaspoon coarse salt
¾ cup cold water

FILLING

¼ pound (1 stick) butter
8 cups chopped onions
2 cups (8½ ounces) grated Gruyère cheese
8 eggs
1 cup cottage cheese
2 cups half-and-half
1 teaspoon coarse salt
½ teaspoon freshly ground black pepper
¼ cup chopped fresh parsley

Lobster Strudels

½ pound (2 sticks) plus 3 tablespoons butter

2 tablespoons unbleached white flour

¾ cup milk

2 teaspoons Dijon mustard

1½ cups sour cream

2 tablespoons capers

2 pounds cooked lobster meat, coarsely chopped

2 tablespoons lime juice

½ cup grated Parmesan cheese

¾ cup chopped chives or scallion greens

½ cup chopped fresh dill

½ teaspoon cayenne

¾ teaspoon freshly ground black pepper

1 teaspoon coarse salt

1 cup bread crumbs

Two 1-pound packages of phyllo dough (22 sheets per pound)

In a small saucepan, melt 3 tablespoons of butter. Add the flour and stir until smooth. Stirring constantly, pour in the milk. Bring the mixture to a boil and cook for 2 minutes. Remove from the heat, and stir in the mustard, sour cream, capers, lobster meat, lime juice, Parmesan, chives or scallions, dill, cayenne, pepper, and salt. Stir well to blend. Chill for 30 minutes.

To make the strudels, you will need 30 sheets of phyllo. Seal and freeze the remaining sheets.

Melt ½ pound of butter in a small saucepan. Place 1 sheet of phyllo on a countertop. Brush lightly with melted butter. Place another sheet of phyllo on top of the first one. Brush with butter and sprinkle with bread crumbs. Repeat, until you have 6 layers, sprinkling every other layer with bread crumbs.

Place one-fifth of the lobster filling along the long edge of the prepared dough. Lifting from the bottom edge to make sure you have all 6 layers, roll the pastry sheets over the filling, jelly-roll fashion. Brush the top with butter, and place on a baking sheet, seam-side down. Repeat this process, until all the dough and filling are used. You should have 5 strudels.

Freeze the strudels for 1½ hours.

Preheat the oven to 400 degrees. Butter a baking sheet.

Remove the strudels from the freezer, and cut each roll into 16 bite-size pieces. Place the pieces on the prepared baking sheet, and bake for 12 to 15 minutes, or until browned and crisp.

Arrange on a platter and serve hot.

YIELD: 80 PIECES.

Mexican Eggs

A fabulous treat to serve at cocktail parties; each bite-size piece is packed with hearty scrambled eggs and spiked with jalapeño pepper, onions, and exotically fragrant coriander leaves.

In a mixing bowl, combine all the ingredients except the eggs and butter. Toss to blend, and set aside.

Hard-boil 24 of the eggs. Cool. Remove and discard the shells. Cut each egg in half, through its equator. Remove the yolk, and save for another use. Cut a little slice off the bottom of each egg white half so it will stand upright. Store the egg white cups, covered, in the refrigerator until ready to use, or up to 1 day.

Shortly before serving, heat the butter in a medium-size skillet. In a bowl, lightly beat the remaining 7 eggs and pour them into the skillet. Scramble the eggs until just firm. Remove from the heat. Stir the scrambled eggs into the tomato-pepper mixture. Spoon a little of this filling into each egg-white cup. Serve warm.

2 tomatoes, centers removed, outer shell finely chopped
1 tablespoon seeded and minced jalapeño pepper
¾ cup finely chopped green bell peppers
¾ cup finely chopped onions
¼ cup finely chopped fresh coriander
1¼ teaspoons coarse salt
½ teaspoon freshly ground black pepper
31 eggs
3 tablespoons butter

YIELD: 48 FILLED EGG CUPS.

Falafel with Cucumber Raita

1 pound dry chick-peas, or 6 cups
    canned
1 cup sesame seeds
8 cloves garlic
3 cups chopped fresh dill
4 cups fresh parsley leaves
5 cups fresh coriander leaves and stems
6 tablespoons lemon juice
1 tablespoon coarse salt
2 teaspoons freshly ground black
    pepper
Peanut oil

CUCUMBER RAITA

2 cups grated cucumber
2 cups plain yogurt
1 teaspoon ground cumin

If using dry chick-peas, place them in a bowl and cover with water by 3 inches. Soak overnight.

Toss the sesame seeds in a skillet over medium heat until lightly browned. Set aside.

Purée the garlic in the bowl of a food processor fitted with a steel blade. Add the dill, parsley, and fresh coriander, and purée again. Add the lemon juice, salt, pepper, and drained chick-peas, and purée until very smooth. The mixture should be moist, but manageable.

Using your hands, shape the mixture into walnut-size patties and flatten slightly. Coat both sides of each patty with the toasted sesame seeds, pressing down lightly so the seeds adhere.

Heat 1 inch of peanut oil in a skillet. Without crowding the pan, fry the falafel in 4 batches, turning each batch once, until nicely browned. Drain on paper towels. Continue until all the falafels are done.

To make the cucumber raita, squeeze the cucumber in paper towels to rid it of excess moisture. Combine the dried cucumber with the yogurt and cumin. Store in a bowl in the refrigerator until ready to serve.

To serve, reheat the falafel in a preheated 375-degree oven for 15 minutes. Arrange the falafels, overlapping, on a platter and serve with the raita on the side.

YIELD: 40 FALAFEL, 4 CUPS RAITA.

Beef and Scallion Rolls

Delicious bite-size treats.

Combine the marinade ingredients in a glass or earthenware dish. Add the meat, turning it in the marinade to coat. Marinate 6 hours or overnight.

Preheat the oven to 400 degrees.

To assemble the rolls, transfer the meat to a cutting board, reserving the marinade. Slice the fillet very thinly into approximately 50 pieces. Press down on each slice with the flat part of a chef's knife, then cut each slightly flattened slice in half, lengthwise. Reserving 1 bunch for garnish, cut the scallions into 2-inch pieces. Roll 1 piece of fillet around 1 or 2 pieces of scallion, and place the roll on a baking sheet. Repeat this process until all the fillet has been used. Brush each roll with some marinade, and roast for 3 to 5 minutes.

Arrange the rolls on a platter, garnish with scallion greens, and serve hot.

YIELD: 100 PIECES.

MARINADE

3 teaspoons minced garlic
½ cup soy sauce
1 tablespoon white vinegar
½ teaspoon freshly ground black pepper
2 tablespoons peanut oil

One 6 to 6½-pound fillet of beef, trimmed
5 bunches of scallions

LABOR DAY—THE LAST HURRAH!
FOR SIXTEEN

CLAM FRITTERS WITH
CHILI-CORIANDER SAUCE

PEARS AND PROSCIUTTO

BLACKFISH WITH
SAFFRON RATATOUILLE

CORN-ON-THE-COB WITH
HERB BUTTER

BITTER GREENS WITH
LEMON VINAIGRETTE

BEER BREAD

PLUM TART

This is the time of year when the corn is so sweet it can be eaten raw right off the stalks. Clams are in abundance. Blackfish is caught fresh every day. Italian prune plums are ripe and ready to be cooked into jams, preserves, or mouth-watering tarts. Pears are beginning to show up at all the fruit stands. With these fabulous treats waiting in store for us, how can we possibly believe that Labor Day is the official ending to our holiday season? It seems to have only just begun.

You can make and freeze the Herb Butter up to 4 weeks in advance.

The Beer Bread can be made up to 1 week ahead of time. Wrap the loaves in foil and freeze. You will need only 2 of the 3 loaves for your party. To serve, place the loaves in their foil inside a preheated 350-degree oven for 15 minutes.

The ratatouille can be made up to 2 days ahead of time and finished just before serving. The dipping sauce for the fritters can be made 2 days ahead and refrigerated.

Assemble the clam fritters up to 1 day in advance if you wish, sauté them the day of the party, and reheat them if necessary in a preheated 350-degree oven for 15 minutes before serving. You can bake the Plum Tarts then, too.

You'll need to buy 6 ripe pears and 6 ounces of thinly sliced prosciutto. Peel, core, and slice the pears into 8 wedges. Wrap each wedge with a slice of prosciutto. This will make 48 pieces.

The salad and its dressing are best when made the day of the party. Lemon juice loses its pizzazz when extracted too far in advance.

Clam Fritters with Chili-Coriander Sauce

Cut the potatoes in half and place in a saucepan. Cover with water and cook until tender, about 18 minutes. Drain. Remove and discard the peel. Mash the potatoes with a fork, and place in a mixing bowl. Add the clams, mozzarella, Parmesan, and 1 tablespoon of flour. Stir to blend. Add the eggs, coriander, scallion greens, salt, red pepper flakes and pepper. Mix thoroughly with your hands.

Dust a baking sheet with ¼ cup of flour. Shape the clam mixture into thirty-two 2 x 1-inch patties. Place them in 1 layer on the baking sheet. Sprinkle the remaining ¼ cup of flour over the patties, cover, and refrigerate for 2 hours or overnight.

To make the sauce, place the jalapeño pepper, garlic, parsley, scallion, greens, and coriander in the bowl of a food processor fitted with a steel blade. Process until the greens are very fine, about 15 seconds. Add the remaining sauce ingredients. Pulse 4 to 5 times, just to blend. Transfer to a bowl and refrigerate until ready to serve.

Heat the peanut oil in a large skillet until almost smoking. Without crowding the pan, sauté the fritters in batches. Cook the fritters 1 minute on each side. Drain on paper towels.

To serve, place the bowl of chili-coriander sauce in the center of a large serving platter. Pile the fritters around the bowl, and garnish with curly parsley. Pass as an appetizer before the buffet.

YIELD: 32 FRITTERS, 1½ CUPS SAUCE.

1 pound baking potatoes
2½ cups raw minced clams, drained
1 cup diced smoked mozzarella
¼ cup grated Parmesan cheese
½ cup plus 1 tablespoon flour
2 eggs
⅓ cup minced fresh coriander leaves
½ cup finely chopped scallion greens
2 teaspoons coarse salt
¾ teaspoon red pepper flakes
1 teaspoon freshly ground black pepper

CHILI-CORIANDER SAUCE

1 tablespoon minced fresh jalapeño pepper
1 teaspoon minced garlic
½ cup chopped fresh parsley
½ cup chopped scallion greens
¼ cup chopped fresh coriander leaves
1 cup mayonnaise
½ cup sour cream
½ teaspoon coarse salt
¼ teaspoon Tabasco

4 cups peanut oil

20 sprigs curly parsley

Blackfish with Saffron Ratatouille

¾ cup olive oil

7 cups chopped onions

2½ cups chopped green peppers

7 teaspoons minced garlic

6 cups peeled and diced baking
potatoes

7 cups diced eggplant (2 large)

7 cups chopped plum tomatoes

1½ tablespoons coarse salt

½ teaspoon red pepper flakes

2 teaspoons saffron

2 teaspoons dried thyme

7 cups chopped zucchini

8 pounds of blackfish fillets, cut into
pieces

½ cup chopped fresh parsley

To make the ratatouille, pour the olive oil into a very large heavy skillet. Add the onions and green peppers, and sauté over low heat until the onions are transparent. Add the garlic, potatoes, eggplant, tomatoes, salt, red pepper flakes, saffron, and thyme. Cover, and simmer for 30 minutes. Add the zucchini and cook 10 minutes more.

Preheat the oven to 425 degrees.

Divide the saffron ratatouille between 2 large oven-to-table casseroles. Cover with foil and bake for 35 minutes. Remove the foil, and distribute the fish evenly over the ratatouille. Cover, and bake 15 minutes more. Sprinkle with parsley and serve.

YIELD: 16 SERVINGS.

Corn-on-the-Cob with Herb Butter

To make the herb butter, combine the softened butter and fresh herbs in a bowl, using a wooden spoon. Transfer to a serving dish, or spoon out onto a sheet of foil lined with plastic wrap and shape into a log 1½ inches in diameter. Wrap and either refrigerate or freeze for later use.

Shortly before serving time, bring a large pot of water to a boil. Add the corn, and simmer until the kernels are cooked but still crisp, about 4 minutes. Serve with the herb butter on the side.

1 pound (4 sticks) butter, softened
¾ cup chopped fresh herbs (use any herb or mixture of herbs you like)
16 ears of corn, peeled and cut in half

YIELD: 16 SERVINGS.

Bitter Greens with Lemon Vinaigrette

Wash and thoroughly dry all the greens. Tear the lettuce into bite-size pieces and place in a large salad bowl. Discarding the stems, add the watercress, arugula, basil, and lemon balm leaves.

Combine the dressing ingredients in a screw-top jar and shake vigorously. When ready to serve, pour the dressing over the greens, and toss to coat.

YIELD: 16 SERVINGS.

¾ pound (1 head) red-leaf lettuce
¾ pound (1 head) Boston lettuce
2½ cups loosely packed watercress
2½ cups loosely packed arugula
2 cups loosely packed small basil leaves
2 cups loosely packed lemon balm or fresh mint leaves

DRESSING
¼ cup lemon juice
¾ cup extra-virgin olive oil
1 egg yolk
2 tablespoons Dijon mustard
1½ teaspoons coarse salt
1 teaspoon freshly ground black pepper

Beer Bread

An excellent bread. This recipe will yield 3 loaves—wrap one in foil and freeze it for a later date. When you're ready to serve, pop the wrapped loaf in a preheated 350-degree oven for 15 minutes.

3 tablespoons active dry yeast
¼ cup sugar
Two 12-ounce bottles of beer
9½ cups unbleached white flour
¼ cup coarse salt
1 egg white, beaten lightly

Pour 1 cup of warm water into a large mixing bowl. Stir in the yeast and sugar. Let stand for 8 to 10 minutes, until the yeast starts to bubble. Add the beer, 4 cups of flour, and the salt. Stir hard for about 10 minutes. Add 5 more cups of flour. Stir to mix well.

Knead the dough on a flour-dusted countertop, using the remaining flour as you go, for about 8 minutes, or until the dough is smooth and elastic. Return the dough to the bowl, cover with a kitchen towel, and let rise in a warm place about 1 to 1½ hours, until doubled in bulk.

Divide and shape the dough into 3 loaves. Place the loaves into 3 buttered 9 x 5-inch pans. Brush the tops with the beaten egg white. Let rise again in a warm place until doubled, about 45 minutes.

Place the loaves in a cold oven, then set the temperature for 350 degrees. Bake for 40 to 45 minutes, or until the loaves sound hollow when lightly tapped. Remove the loaves from their pans, and cool on a wire rack.

YIELD: 3 LOAVES.

Plum Tart

Perfect for this time of year. The plums are ripe and juicy, and the tart is a really satisfying finish to a perfect dinner.

Preheat the oven to 400 degrees.

Combine the flour, walnuts, and sugar in a large bowl. Add the butter and the egg yolks. Mix, either by hand or with an electric mixer, until crumbly.

Press 3 cups of the crumb mixture, in 1 even layer, into each bottom of two 9½-inch springform pans. Arrange the plums in the pans, skin-side down, beginning from the outer edge and forming a flower pattern.

Sprinkle the rest of the crumb mixture evenly over the plums.

Bake the tarts for 40 to 50 minutes, or until lightly browned and the plum juice has risen to the top. Remove from the oven and cool for 10 minutes. Remove from the pans and transfer the tarts to flat cake plates.

Serve warm or at room temperature.

4 cups unbleached white flour
1½ cups finely chopped walnuts
1½ cups light brown sugar
¾ pound (3 sticks) cold butter, cut into 24 pieces
2 egg yolks
4 pounds fresh, ripe Italian prune plums, pitted and quartered lengthwise

YIELD: 2 TARTS, 8 TO 10 SERVINGS EACH.

AUTUMN'S HARVEST

LUNCH ON A COOL FALL DAY FOR EIGHT

A GRAND HARVEST FOR TWENTY-FOUR

INDIAN SUMMER LUNCH FOR TWELVE

A SPECIAL-OCCASION DINNER FOR EIGHT

AN ELEGANT DINNER FOR TWELVE

THANKSGIVING FOR TWELVE

SUNDAY AFTERNOON TEA FOR TEN TO TWELVE

This Autumn section involved planning adaptable meals that could be served indoors or out.

The Grand Harvest for twenty-four is the kind of meal that can be enjoyed outside, around a large picnic table covered with a crisp tablecloth, or as a casual meal set up indoors as a buffet.

Lunch on a Cool Fall Day is perfect fare for indoors. However, if the sun suddenly makes an unscheduled appearance, this meal can easily move to your patio or terrace.

Sunday Afternoon Tea is exquisite outdoors. My husband set up a hammock between two copper beech trees, and invariably our guests gravitate there, to stretch out and appreciate the last rays of rosy sun, enjoying whatever is left of an autumn afternoon.

In using the freshest produce available, we have created dishes that naturally conform to the seasonal changes in color. At the beginning of autumn we can decorate our tables with fresh garden flowers, but by the end of the season, we are able to replace them with the flashy colors of fall: a cluster of squashes surrounding a bright pumpkin; intoxicating bouquets of dazzling yellow, red, and orange leaves, which beautifully grace our mantelpieces; the subtle beauty of Indian corn joined with shafts of dry wheat make a welcoming decoration for any front door; ample bowls of orchard-fresh apples, pears, and nuts to freshen our tables.

It's a season that begins with parties around an outdoor grill, and ends with friends gathered around a hearth.

LUNCH ON A COOL FALL DAY
FOR EIGHT

TOMATO-LEEK SOUP

DUCK PIE

WATERCRESS AND MUSHROOM
SALAD WITH
BALSAMIC DRESSING

PEARS POACHED IN
WHITE WINE

This is an easy and rewarding lunch to serve on one of those crisp autumn afternoons. Much of it can be made assembled well ahead of time, leaving you to relax with the company of your friends.

The Tomato-Leek Soup, for instance, can be made up to 2 days in advance and reheated before the party.

The Pears Poached in White Wine can also be prepared 2 days ahead and stored, covered, in the refrigerator until the morning of your lunch. To enjoy them at their best, this dessert should be served at room temperature. Since autumn is pear season, you'll have a wide variety to choose from. Make certain to select pears that are almost ready to eat. By this I mean fragrant, but still a bit firm.

The Duck Pie cannot be baked ahead of time; however, it can be assembled, then covered tightly in plastic wrap and frozen. The pie will need to be defrosted the morning of the party and baked according to the instructions in the recipe.

When preparing the duck, save the bones and store them in the freezer for your next stockpot. Duck fat, refrigerated in a tightly covered container, can last almost indefinitely. It is superb when used in almost any white bean dish, such as cassoulet or stew. It lends a very special flavor to cabbage dishes and is perfect for roasting potatoes. If you'd like to try Swedish potatoes, combine the duck fat with sliced potatoes in a covered saucepan, and simmer over medium heat until done. What a treat!

Tomato-Leek Soup

Melt the butter in a heavy saucepan. Add the onion and leeks, and sauté over low heat for 15 minutes, making sure the onion does not brown. Stir in the garlic and flour, and mix well. Add the chicken stock, wine, tomatoes, pepper, salt, bay leaf, allspice, thyme, and parsley sprigs. Bring to a boil, adjust the heat, and simmer, covered, for 30 minutes.

Remove and discard the tied parsley. Add the heavy cream and blue cheese, and stir until the cheese is melted. Reheat and serve in deep soup plates garnished with parsley.

YIELD: 3 QUARTS, 8 TO 10 SERVINGS.

4 tablespoons butter
2 cups minced onions
4 leeks, sliced fine (use white and light green parts)
2 teaspoons minced garlic
3 tablespoons unbleached white flour
7 cups chicken stock (page 8)
½ cup dry white wine
4 pounds (about 2½ cups) fresh tomatoes, peeled and finely chopped
1 teaspoon freshly ground black pepper
1½ teaspoons coarse salt
1 bay leaf
⅛ teaspoon ground allspice
¾ teaspoon dried thyme
10 fresh parsley sprigs, with stems, tied with cotton string
¾ cup heavy cream
1½ ounces blue cheese
2 tablespoons minced fresh parsley

Duck Pie

The green peppercorns, Madeira wine, sage, and nutmeg infuse this classic dish with just the right amount of spice to make it extra special.

CRUST

2½ cups unbleached white flour
12 tablespoons (1½ sticks) cold butter, cut into small pieces
½ teaspoon coarse salt
½ teaspoon freshly ground black pepper
2 tablespoons lemon juice
⅓ cup cold water

FILLING

One 4½-pound duck
1 pound fresh, lean pork, coarsely ground
2 tablespoons butter
½ cup minced shallots
1 teaspoon minced garlic
¼ cup strong chicken stock (page 8)
¼ cup Madeira wine
1 teaspoon ground sage
1 tablespoon drained green peppercorns
¼ teaspoon freshly grated nutmeg
1½ teaspoons freshly ground black pepper
1 tablespoon coarse salt
1 cup sour cream

1 egg yolk
1 tablespoon milk

To make the crust, place the flour in a food processor bowl fitted with a steel blade. Add the butter, salt, and pepper. Pulse 5 times. Add the lemon juice and cold water and process for 30 seconds. Turn the mixture out onto a lightly floured countertop. Gather the pastry into a ball, cover with plastic wrap, and chill for 30 minutes.

To make the filling, remove all the meat from the duck and cut into ½-inch pieces, discarding the skin. Place the duck meat in a bowl. Mince the duck liver and add it to the meat, along with the ground pork.

Melt the butter in a large sauté pan, add the shallots, and sauté for 2 minutes over low heat. Add the garlic and the meat mixture and stir quickly, breaking up the meat with a wooden spoon. Add the chicken stock, Madeira, sage, peppercorns, nutmeg, pepper, and salt. Turn the heat to high, and cook the mixture for 10 minutes, stirring occasionally. Remove from the heat. Fold in the sour cream, and cool to room temperature.

Preheat the oven to 425 degrees.

To assemble the pie, roll two-thirds of the pastry into a 12-inch circle, ⅛ inch thick. Line a buttered 10-inch springform pan with the pastry, pressing it 1 inch up the sides. Spoon the meat evenly into the pastry shell. Roll the remaining pastry into a 10-inch round. Cover the top of the pie with it. Using a fork, press around the edge of the pie to seal it. Cut a few slits into the top crust. Beat the egg yolk with the milk and brush this over the entire surface to create a glaze.

Bake 10 minutes. Lower the oven temperature to 350, and bake for another 40 minutes. Place the pie on a rack and let it cool for at least 30 minutes before serving. This will allow it to set. Serve warm, or at room temperature.

YIELD: 8 SERVINGS.

Watercress and Mushroom Salad with Balsamic Dressing

Combine the watercress, mushrooms, and onion slices in a salad bowl.

Combine the dressing ingredients in a screw-top jar and shake vigorously. Pour over the salad, toss gently, and serve.

YIELD: 8 SERVINGS.

4½ cups (2 bunches) loosely packed watercress, large stems removed
10 fresh mushrooms, thinly sliced
½ red onion, thinly sliced

DRESSING

2 tablespoons Balsamic vinegar
6 tablespoons olive oil
½ teaspoon coarse salt
¼ teaspoon freshly ground black pepper

Pears Poached in White Wine

Mix the wine, water, sugar, vanilla bean, and lemon peel in a large saucepan and bring to a boil. Remove from the heat.

Peel and core the pears, leaving the stems intact. Place the pears in the hot wine mixture and bring to a boil. Lower the heat until the liquid is simmering and poach the pears, covered, for 15 minutes, or until just tender. Test their doneness by inserting a sharp knife in the center of the pear; there should be no resistance. Remove from the heat, and allow to cool in the saucepan.

Place each pear, stem up, on an individual plate. Spoon the white wine syrup over them, and garnish each one with a fresh mint sprig.

NOTE: The pears can be stored in a covered bowl in the refrigerator for up to 1 week, and served at room temperature.

YIELD: 8 SERVINGS.

2½ cups dry white wine
2½ cups water
1½ cups sugar
½ vanilla bean, cut in half lengthwise
Peel of 1 lemon, cut into strips
8 D'anjou or Bartlett pears
8 fresh mint sprigs

A GRAND HARVEST
FOR TWENTY-FOUR

ROAST LOIN OF PORK
WITH HOT BLACK MUSTARD

CABBAGE ROLLS IN
TOMATO SAUCE

BOILED NEW POTATOES
WITH PARSLEY

CHICORY AND ARUGULA SALAD

BLACK PEPPER–WALNUT
BISCUITS WITH STILTON
AND SEEDLESS GREEN GRAPES

PIKANTE EINGELEGTE KÜRBIS
(PICKLED PUMPKIN)

THREE GLAZED
APPLE TARTS WITH
CRÈME FRAÎCHE

Autumn brings a bountiful supply of vegetables and fruits that can add a brand new dimension to all your menus. We're fortunate to be located next to a potato field, and are delighted when the harvesting begins. The earthy aroma of new potatoes is in itself an inspiration. This is also the season for succulent, vine-ripened tomatoes, leeks, sweet cabbages, and cauliflower. Freshly picked apples and pears are in abundance, as well as pumpkins and a wide variety of juicy melons.

The following menu is a wonderful and comparatively easy way for welcoming in the season.

The Pickled Pumpkin (Pikante Eingelegte Kürbis) should be prepared 3 days ahead and allowed to marinate in the brine until the day of the party. This is an excellent side dish, adding just the right piquancy to the subtle taste of pork.

The Cabbage Rolls can also be made 2 days in advance and refrigerated. To reheat, place them, covered, in a 350-degree oven for 30 minutes, and serve.

The salad should be rinsed, dried, and chilled in the refrigerator the morning of the lunch and assembled at the last minute. The dressing, too, can be made earlier and kept refrigerated until needed.

The Black Pepper–Walnut Biscuits should be made the morning of the party and served slightly warm. Pile them in a lovely bowl and place them next to a platter of chilled seedless green grapes and a crock of Stilton cheese. It's a winning combination that's great for any buffet.

All that's left for you to prepare is the Roast Loin of Pork with Hot Black Mustard, Boiled New Potatoes with Parsley, and the scrumptious tart.

It's best to time the cooking of the pork loin and the new potatoes so they are done 15 minutes prior to the meal. This will leave 10 minutes for the meat to rest before it is sliced, garnished, and served.

Hot black mustard is available in most gourmet shops, or try the fine foods section of your grocery store. If you cannot find this particular type of mustard, try making your own. Mix together ¾ cup of grainy mustard with 1 teaspoon of chili powder and 1 teaspoon paprika. It'll give the loin the same desired taste.

To appreciate the Apple Tart at its very best, it should be served warm from the oven, with crème fraîche on the side. There is nothing quite like it to finish off this hearty meal.

Roast Loin of Pork with Hot Black Mustard

3 tablespoons butter, softened

4 cups finely chopped onions

3 teaspoons minced garlic

1 tablespoon ground sage

1 tablespoon coarse salt

2 teaspoons freshly ground black pepper

One 6-ounce jar hot black mustard

Three 2½-pound boneless loins of pork

¾ cup dry white wine

1 cup chicken stock (page 8)

1 bunch watercress sprigs

Preheat the oven to 375 degrees.

Butter the bottom of a large roasting pan, and sprinkle the onions and garlic evenly over it.

Combine the sage, salt, pepper, and hot black mustard in a small bowl. Rub each pork loin with one-third of the mixture. Place the meat on the bed of onions, making sure the loins don't touch.

Roast 30 minutes, uncovered. Remove from the oven, pour the wine and chicken stock around the pork loins, and roast 20 minutes longer.

Remove from the oven and allow the meat to rest in a warm place, covered, for 10 minutes. Discard the onions, and transfer the pork loin to a cutting board, slice, and arrange the pieces on a warm serving platter. Garnish with the sprigs of watercress.

YIELD: 24 SERVINGS.

Cabbage Rolls in Tomato Sauce

*A basic dish, spiked with Tabasco and blanketed with a sauce made
from the ripest, sweetest tomatoes, not only is this a superb addition to any buffet, it is also wonderful as a first course, or as a
light meal served with a small green salad and masses of crunchy
French bread.*

To make the sauce, heat the olive oil in a large saucepan.
Add the onions and garlic and sauté for 2 minutes. Add the
tomatoes with their juices and the remaining sauce ingredients. Stir to combine. Bring to a boil, and simmer, covered,
for 20 minutes.

Place the cabbage in a large pot, cover with water, and
bring to a boil. Simmer 8 to 10 minutes, until the cabbage is
tender. Drain and set aside.

For the filling, heat the olive oil in a skillet and sauté the
onions for 5 minutes. Add the garlic and sauté 2 minutes
more. Transfer to a mixing bowl and add the ground lamb,
cumin, salt, pepper, bread crumbs, and eggs. Mix with your
hands.

Preheat the oven to 350 degrees.

Ladle a thin layer of tomato sauce over the bottom of a
large buttered roasting pan.

To make the cabbage rolls, gently remove the larger outer
leaves and shave off the thicker part of the stem. As the leaves
become smaller you will need two for each roll.

Place ⅓ cup of filling in the center of a cabbage leaf. Fold
the sides of the leaf over the meat and roll it up. Place each
roll on the roasting pan, seam-side down. Repeat this process
until all the filling has been used.

Ladle the remaining sauce over the cabbage rolls and bake,
covered, for 45 minutes. Uncover, and bake another 15 minutes.

NOTE: The cabbage rolls freeze well for up to 6 months.
When ready to serve, defrost and reheat, uncovered, in a 350-
degree oven.

YIELD: 40 ROLLS; SERVES 24 AS PART OF A BUFFET.

SAUCE

¼ cup olive oil
6 cups finely chopped onions
2 tablespoons minced garlic
6 pounds fresh plum tomatoes, or 6
    pounds canned plum tomatoes,
    drained and coarsely chopped
3 cups chicken stock (page 8)
2 teaspoons dried thyme
1 tablespoon dried basil
2 bay leaves
2 cups chopped fresh parsley
1 tablespoon ground cumin
1 teaspoon Tabasco
1 tablespoon red wine vinegar
1 tablespoon coarse salt
1 tablespoon freshly ground black
    pepper

CABBAGE AND FILLING

3 heads savoy or green cabbage, cut in
    half
¼ cup olive oil
2 cups finely chopped onions
3 teaspoons minced garlic
4 pounds lean ground lamb
1½ teaspoons ground cumin
2 tablespoons coarse salt
2 tablespoons freshly ground black
    pepper
1½ cups bread crumbs
4 eggs

Boiled New Potatoes with Parsley

8 pounds new potatoes, scrubbed
1 teaspoon coarse salt
1 cup finely chopped fresh parsley

Cover the new potatoes with cold water in a large saucepan. Add the salt and bring to a boil. Simmer over low heat 12 to 15 minutes, or until tender when pierced with a fork. Drain the potatoes and transfer to a large heated serving bowl.

Garnish with chopped parsley.

YIELD: 24 SERVINGS.

Chicory and Arugula Salad

4 pounds chicory (approximately 3 heads), cut into bite-size pieces
8 cups loosely packed (approximately 4 bunches) arugula leaves
1 large red onion, peeled and cut into thin rings

Combine the chicory, arugula, and red onion in a large bowl.

Mash the garlic and salt to a paste and place in a screw-top jar with the other dressing ingredients. Screw on the lid and shake vigorously. When ready to serve, pour the dressing over the salad and toss well.

YIELD: 24 SERVINGS.

DRESSING

1 clove garlic
2 teaspoons coarse salt
½ cup sherry wine vinegar
¼ teaspoon cayenne
1 tablespoon Dijon mustard
1¼ cups olive oil

Black Pepper—Walnut Biscuits with Stilton and Seedless Green Grapes

This combination is a wonderful addition to any buffet. My family also enjoys it as a light lunch or late-night snack.

Preheat the oven to 400 degrees.

Place the flour, baking powder, butter, and black pepper in the bowl of an electric mixer. Mix at medium speed until crumbly. Turn off the mixer and add the eggs. With the motor running, add the half-and-half and mix just to blend; do not overmix, or the dough will become tough. Fold in the walnuts by hand.

Transfer the dough to a lightly floured surface. With your hands, shape into a rectangle 13 x 18 inches, approximately ½ inch thick. Cut into 2½-inch squares or, for appetizer size, cut into 1-inch squares.

Place the squares on a lightly buttered baking sheet. Brush each piece with the beaten egg. Bake 20 to 25 minutes, until golden. Serve warm, with a wedge of Stilton cheese and chilled seedless green grapes.

NOTE: Leftover biscuits can be frozen for up to 3 months. To reheat, place the frozen biscuits on a baking sheet in a preheated 350-degree oven for 15 minutes.

4 cups unbleached white flour

2 teaspoons baking powder

¾ pound cold butter (3 sticks), cut into small pieces

2 tablespoons freshly ground black pepper

4 eggs

1½ cups half-and-half

1½ cups coarsely chopped walnuts

1 egg, lightly beaten

YIELD: APPROXIMATELY THIRTY 2½-INCH SQUARES, OR SEVENTY-FIVE 1-INCH SQUARES.

Pikant Eingelegte Kürbis (Pickled Pumpkin)

This versatile side dish needs to marinate for 2 days before it can be served. Piquant and slightly crunchy, it beautifully complements poultry and game dishes as well as pork.

1 medium pumpkin (approximately 8 pounds whole)
2 cups distilled white vinegar
6 cups sugar
1½ cups cider vinegar
1 cup water
6 whole cloves
Peel of ½ lemon, cut into strips
⅔ cup orange juice

Cut the pumpkin in half. Scrape out and discard the seeds. Peel the pumpkin and cut into 2 x 1½-inch pieces. Combine the pumpkin, white vinegar, and 2 cups of water in an earthenware bowl. Refrigerate for 12 hours, or overnight.

Drain the pumpkin and discard the liquid.

Combine the sugar, cider vinegar, water, cloves, and lemon peel in a large saucepan, and bring to a boil. Add the pumpkin, and simmer, covered, for about 30 minutes. Stir occasionally. The pumpkin is done when it is glossy and can be pierced easily with a knife. Saving the cooking liquid, transfer the pumpkin to an earthenware crock or large glass jar.

Add the orange juice to the cooking liquid and bring to a rolling boil. Pour the liquid over the pumpkin. Tightly cover the crock or jar with plastic wrap and store in a cool, dark place. Refrigerated, it will keep up to 3 months.

YIELD: 24 SERVINGS, APPROXIMATELY 12 TO 13 CUPS.

Three Glazed Apple Tarts with Crème Fraîche

Place the flour, 3 tablespoons of sugar, 18 tablespoons of butter, and all the margarine in a large bowl; blend with your hands until it resembles coarse meal.

In a small bowl, beat together the egg yolks, lemon juice, and cold water. Pour over the flour mixture, and using your hands, combine the ingredients until the dough holds together to form a ball. Cover the dough in plastic wrap and refrigerate for 30 minutes.

Preheat the oven to 450 degrees.

Grease 3 cookie sheets measuring 12 x 17 x 1 inches.

Divide the dough into 3 equal parts. Roll out each part into an 11-inch circle, approximately ⅛ inch thick. To transfer the dough circle, drape it over the rolling pin, and unroll it onto the prepared cookie sheet. Repeat this process with the remaining 2 pieces of dough.

Peel, halve, and core the apples. Place the halves, cut side down, on a cutting board. Slice each half thinly. Arrange 12 sliced apple halves on each pastry circle, fanning the slices so that the pastry is completely covered. Repeat this process with the remaining 2 pastries.

Melt the remaining 6 tablespoons of butter in a small saucepan, and evenly brush the 3 tarts with it. Sprinkle each tart with ½ cup of sugar.

Bake 30 minutes, or until the crusts are browned and the apples tender.

Transfer the warm apple tarts to 3 large cake plates. Serve with crème fraîche on the side.

6 cups unbleached white flour

1½ cups plus 3 tablespoons sugar

24 tablespoons (3 sticks) cold butter

20 tablespoons (2½ sticks) cold margarine

3 egg yolks

3 tablespoons lemon juice

¾ cup cold water

7½ pounds (about 18 large) McIntosh apples

3 cups crème fraîche (page 9)

YIELD: 3 TARTS, 24 SERVINGS.

INDIAN SUMMER LUNCH
FOR TWELVE

BELLINI
CHAMPAGNE COCKTAILS

FIGS AND MELON WITH
GOAT CHEESE AND MINT

GRILLED TUNA IN A
SESAME MARINADE

TOMATO-ONION SAUTÉ

FRENCH BREAD

ORANGE MOUSSE WITH
CRÈME CHANTILLY

BUTTERSCOTCH BROWNIES

The wonderful thing about this lunch is that although it is planned as an outdoor barbecue, if the weather conspires against you, the party can easily be moved inside. The tuna steaks will turn out almost as well grilled under your broiler as they would over hot coals. I would suggest that you make both the Orange Mousse and the Butterscotch Brownies the day before. Everything else can be prepared the day of the party.

Don't marinate the tuna steaks for more than 4 hours. The sesame and garlic might overpower its delicate taste. Time the lunch so that the tuna is served within an hour after it's cooked.

When you're shopping for goat cheese, remember to follow this simple rule: Freshest is best! With goat cheese becoming such a growing industry, farmers have begun to send infant cheeses packed in dry ice through United Parcel Service, so that many stores receive their precious cargos in perfect condition. Plump purple figs look wonderful with the impeccably white cheese and rich orange cantaloupe, accented with sprigs of fresh mint. Serve this with lots of crusty French bread, warm from the oven.

The Tomato-Onion Sauté takes only minutes to prepare, so save this for last since it should be served hot.

This meal makes a beautiful buffet. The only thing left to do is to treat yourself to a Bellini Cocktail: 1 part strained peach juice to 2 parts champagne.

Grilled Tuna in a Sesame Marinade

You can substitute chicken for the tuna. Leftovers in both cases make a fabulous luncheon salad, mixed with fresh crisp greens and a lemon vinaigrette.

Place the marinade ingredients in a glass dish large enough to hold all 12 pieces of fish comfortably. Add the tuna, making sure it is completely covered with the marinade. Marinate, covered, at room temperature for 1 hour. If you prefer to marinate the fish in the refrigerator, do so, but not for more than 4 hours. Longer than that would cause the marinade to overpower the delicate taste of the tuna.

Light the grill. When the coals are almost white, grill the tuna about 3 to 4 minutes on each side. To broil, place the fish under a preheated broiler about 3 inches from the heat source, and grill for 4 minutes on each side.

Heat the marinade in a small saucepan on the side of the grill. Serve the tuna with a little marinade spooned over each piece.

YIELD: 12 SERVINGS.

SESAME MARINADE

½ cup Chinese Sesame oil
¾ cup soy sauce
¼ cup lime juice
¾ cup olive oil
5 teaspoons minced garlic
1 teaspoon red hot pepper flakes
1 cup water

6 pounds fresh tuna, cut into 12 pieces about ¾-inch thick

Tomato-Onion Sauté

Plump red and yellow tomatoes flecked with green make this a cheerfully bright addition to any meal.

⅓ cup olive oil
2 red onions, sliced into thin rings
2 teaspoons minced garlic
2½ pounds cherry tomatoes
2½ pounds very small yellow plum tomatoes
¼ cup chopped fresh chives
1½ teaspoons salt
1 teaspoon freshly ground black pepper
2 cups whole fresh basil leaves

Heat the olive oil in a sauté pan. Add the onions and sauté over medium heat for about 5 minutes, or until the onions are soft. Add the garlic, and sauté for 2 minutes more. Turn the heat to medium-high, add the red and yellow tomatoes and sauté about 5 minutes, shaking the pan a few times. Don't stir with a utensil, as this will break the skins. The tomatoes should be hot, skins unbroken. Transfer them to a heated serving dish and sprinkle with chives, salt, and pepper. Distribute the basil leaves evenly over the top and serve hot.

YIELD: 12 SERVINGS.

Orange Mousse with Crème Chantilly

Place lemon juice in a measuring cup and add enough orange juice to make 2 cups juice in all. Combine the juices and gelatin in a medium-size saucepan. Let the gelatin soften, about 5 minutes.

Place the egg yolks and sugar in the bowl of an electric mixer and cream until light and fluffy. Add to the juice-gelatin mixture, and cook over medium heat, stirring constantly, until the liquid begins to thicken and coats a wooden spoon. Do not boil, or the eggs will curdle and the custard base will be ruined. Remove from the heat and stir in the orange peel and the Grand Marnier. Transfer to a mixing bowl and chill until the custard has set to the consistency of unbeaten egg whites.

Beat the egg whites until soft peaks hold. Fold into the partly chilled custard. Whip the cream until soft peaks hold. Fold into the custard. Pour the mousse in a serving bowl and chill in the refrigerator about 3 hours.

When ready to serve, whip the cream, confectioners' sugar, and vanilla until the beater leaves light traces on the surface of the cream. Serve the Crème Chantilly in a separate bowl, placed next to the mousse.

NOTE: Covered and refrigerated, the Orange Mousse will keep up to a week.

6 tablespoons lemon juice
Orange juice
3 tablespoons unflavored gelatin
8 egg yolks
2 cups sugar
3 tablespoons grated orange peel
2 tablespoons Grand Marnier
4 egg whites
4 cups heavy cream

CRÈME CHANTILLY

2 cups heavy cream
2 tablespoons confectioners' sugar
Seeds from half a vanilla bean

YIELD: 12 TO 14 SERVINGS.

Butterscotch Brownies

A quick and simple recipe for a truly delicious brownie.

8 tablespoons (1 stick) butter
2 cups (1 pound) dark brown sugar
1 teaspoon vanilla extract
1 teaspoon instant espresso
2 eggs
1¼ cups unbleached white flour
½ teaspoon baking powder
1 cup finely chopped walnuts
⅔ cup chocolate chips

Preheat the oven to 350 degrees.

Melt the butter in a heavy saucepan over low heat. Stirring constantly, add the sugar and cook until smooth, about 5 minutes. Remove from the heat, and let cool for 15 minutes. Put it into the bowl of an electric mixer, add the vanilla, espresso, and the eggs, and beat for 2 minutes. Add the flour, baking powder, walnuts, and chocolate chips. Mix at low speed until well blended.

Scrape the batter into a buttered 13 x 9 x 2-inch baking pan. Smooth the surface. Bake 30 minutes. Remove from the oven. Lightly shake the pan. If the batter moves, return the pan to the oven and bake 5 minutes more. When done, the brownies should be set on the outside and slightly moist on the inside. Cool, and cut into 24 bars.

Transfer the bars to a plate. Cover tightly with plastic wrap and store them in the refrigerator. They will stay moist for up to 3 days.

YIELD: 24 BROWNIES.

A SPECIAL-OCCASION DINNER
FOR EIGHT

This is an elegant lobster dinner that requires no bibs, no finger bowls, and no tools. All the work is done in the kitchen well before the guests arrive. Although the preparation needs to be done the day of the party, the menu has been organized to make it as easy and manageable as possible.

The Autumn-Fruit Pie can be baked 3 to 4 hours before the party and warmed just before it's served.

The salad ingredients can be washed, dried, and chilled in the morning, and assembled at the last minute. The dressing can be made in the morning and refrigerated. Try to find authentic, aged Parmesan (Reggiano Parmesan), there is really nothing quite like it.

It would be a great time saver to julienne the celeriac and zucchini in a food processor fitted with the proper attachment. It goes lightning quick this way.

The lobster can be cooked, the meat removed, cut into pieces, and returned to the shells, 2 hours before you need to bake them. The Saffron Sauce, too, can be made ahead and reheated when you need it. Store both, covered, in the refrigerator.

The Baked Potato Slices and vegetables are easy to do an hour ahead and finished just before serving.

Candlelight, fall flowers, soft music, lobster, and a great champagne . . . what could be more sensational?

CAESAR SALAD
LOAVES AND FISHES

LOBSTER WITH
SAFFRON SAUCE

BAKED POTATO SLICES

SAUTÉED CELERIAC
AND ZUCCHINI

AUTUMN FRUIT PIE
WITH WHIPPED CREAM

Caesar Salad Loaves and Fishes

A classic favorite that can be served any time of the year.

1½ teaspoons coarse salt
1 large clove garlic, peeled
3 heads Romaine lettuce
3 flat anchovies, minced
1 tablespoon of the anchovy oil
⅓ cup grated Parmesan cheese
3 tablespoons fresh lemon juice
⅓ cup extra-virgin olive oil
¾ teaspoon freshly ground black
   pepper
1 loaf French bread
Olive oil for brushing the bread

Sprinkle the salt into an earthenware bowl. Rub the bottom and sides with the clove of garlic, pressing firmly. Discard the clove.

Choose only the smaller inner leaves for the salad, saving the large outer leaves for another use. Place the leaves in the salad bowl. Add the anchovies, anchovy oil, and Parmesan. Sprinkle with lemon juice, olive oil, and pepper; toss gently but thoroughly.

Preheat the oven to 400 degrees.

Slice the French Bread into ½-inch-thick pieces. Lightly brush each piece with olive oil, place on a baking sheet, and bake 7 to 8 minutes.

Divide the salad among 8 plates, place 2 slices of bread on each plate, and serve as a first course.

YIELD: 8 SERVINGS.

Lobster with Saffron Sauce

Morsels of tender white lobster, piled into their crimson shells, gentled by a yellowy Saffron Sauce are a perfect blending of colors, textures, and tastes.

Fill a 20-quart pot with 5 quarts of water and bring to a boil. Plunge the lobsters into the water; you may have to do this in 2 or 3 batches. Cook them for 6 minutes. Remove, and set aside until they are cool enough to handle.

Since you'll be serving the lobster in its shell, be careful when you split them in half. Try not to cut all the way through. Remove the meat from the tails and claws and place on a cutting board. Rinse the tail and body of each shell, discarding the claw shell but leaving the smaller legs intact. Dry with a towel and place the shells cut-side up in a buttered roasting pan. Slice the lobster meat into bite-size pieces and return them to the shells.

In a heavy saucepan, melt the butter. Add the shallots, and sauté over low heat for 2 minutes. Stir in the flour, continuing to stir while adding the fish stock, white wine, saffron, pepper, and Tabasco. Bring the mixture to a boil. Simmer, uncovered, over low heat for 10 minutes. Add the cream, and simmer 10 minutes more. Pour the sauce through a strainer into another saucepan.

Preheat the oven to 375 degrees.

Fifteen minutes before serving time, bake the lobsters, covered, for 10 minutes. Using two large spoons, transfer each lobster onto its own heated dinner plate. Bring the sauce to a boil and ladle a spoonful over each lobster. The rest of the sauce can be poured into a sauceboat and passed separately.

Garnish each lobster with chopped parsley and serve.

Eight 1½-pound live lobsters
6 tablespoons butter
½ cup minced shallots
2½ tablespoons unbleached white flour
2 cups fish stock
¼ cup dry white wine
1 teaspoon saffron
½ teaspoon freshly ground white pepper
⅛ teaspoon Tabasco
½ cup heavy cream
2 tablespoons chopped fresh parsley

YIELD: 8 SERVINGS.

Baked Potato Slices

This is such an easy and satisfying way to bake potatoes that you may find yourself using this method over and over again.

½ cup olive oil
4 pounds (approximately 6 large) potatoes, peeled
1½ teaspoons coarse salt
¾ teaspoon freshly ground black pepper

Preheat the oven to 400 degrees.

Brush a 17 x 13-inch baking pan with 2 tablespoons of the olive oil.

Slice the potatoes ⅛ inch thick. Place them in a mixing bowl, add the remaining olive oil, salt, and pepper. Toss to coat the potato slices.

Line the baking pan with the slightly overlapping potato slices.

Bake 20 minutes, or until potatoes are crisp on the outside and tender on the inside. Serve on the same plate with the lobster.

YIELD: 8 SERVINGS.

Sautéed Celeriac and Zucchini

3 tablespoons olive oil
2 pounds (2 heads) celeriac, peeled and cut into 2 x ¼-inch julienne
1¾ pounds (4 small) zucchini, cut into 2 x ¼-inch julienne
1 teaspoon coarse salt
½ teaspoon freshly ground black pepper

Heat the olive oil in a large skillet. Add the julienned celeriac, and sauté for 5 minutes. Add the zucchini, and sauté 3 minutes more. Season with salt and pepper.

Serve on the same plate with the lobster.

YIELD: 8 SERVINGS.

Autumn Fruit Pie with Whipped Cream

Freshly picked fragrant pears, apples straight from the orchard, the robust taste of dried prunes, a hint of ginger. A fabulous pie that, when served warm with a dollop of whipped cream, becomes a memorable dessert!

Preheat the oven to 375 degrees.

To make the crust, place 2 cups of flour and the cold butter in a food processor bowl fitted with a metal blade; pulse 5 times. Add the egg yolk and cold water; pulse 10 times. Scrape the dough onto a lightly floured countertop. Gather it into a ball and let it rest, covered and refrigerated, while you prepare the filling.

To make the filling, combine the prunes, ½ cup of sugar, and the wine in a heavy saucepan. Cover, and cook over a low heat for 10 minutes. Transfer the prunes with their liquid into a large mixing bowl. Add the pears, apples, ginger, lemon peel, lemon juice, and flour, and mix thoroughly.

Roll two-thirds of the dough into a circle 14 inches in diameter and ⅛ inch thick. Fit the circle into a 10-inch buttered pie plate, and trim the edges. Spoon the fruit filling into the pastry shell. Gather the leftover trimmings into the remaining dough, and roll into a 10-inch circle. Cover the pie, and flute the edges. Cut a few slits in the top crust, brush with melted butter, and sprinkle with the remaining 2 tablespoons sugar.

Bake 45 to 50 minutes, or until golden brown.

Serve warm, or at room temperature. The cream, confectioners' sugar, and vanilla can be whipped ahead of time, placed in a bowl, and passed separately.

YIELD: 8 SERVINGS.

CRUST

2 cups unbleached white flour

9 tablespoons cold butter, cut into small pieces

1 egg yolk

¼ cup cold water

FRUIT FILLING

20 pitted prunes

½ cup plus 2 tablespoons sugar

½ cup medium dry wine

2 pears, peeled, cored, and cut into thin wedges

3 tart apples, peeled, cored, and cut into thin wedges

2 tablespoons peeled and minced fresh gingerroot

1½ teaspoons grated lemon peel

1½ tablespoons lemon juice

2 tablespoons unbleached white flour

2 tablespoons butter, melted

1 cup heavy cream

2 tablespoons confectioners' sugar

Seeds of ½ vanilla bean

AN ELEGANT DINNER
FOR TWELVE

We've devised this soothing, yet elegant meal for an evening late in the autumn season, when you just get the first whiff of winter. Although this dinner must be prepared the same day as the party, everything, except the soufflé, can be readied a few hours before.

The mussels, for instance, can be boiled, placed on a baking sheet in their half shells, and broiled at the last minute.

The chicken breasts can be filled and browned 2 hours ahead. Once cooked meat is refrigerated, it loses moisture and tenderness, so I recommend that you leave the browned chicken at room temperature until ready to bake. That process will take only 30 minutes. The sauce, too, can be made at that time, and reheated when you're ready to serve the chicken. The green beans can be blanched ahead of time, then sautéed in the butter while the chicken breasts are baking.

Rice is an excellent side dish to this entrée. I have suggested Wehani Basmati Rice, which is a dark brown rice with its natural skin intact. It has a wonderfully nutty taste that beautifully complements the mushroom stuffing in the chicken.

Since the apricot purée mixture needs 1 hour to chill, you can complete the first step of the dessert recipe early in the day. If you're using one soufflé dish, the dessert will have to bake for at least 35 to 40 minutes. If you're using ramekins, the baking time will be less, so plan accordingly. Whisk the whipped cream at the last minute. This dessert is a winner, and once you get the hang of it, I'm certain you will want to serve it often!

Broiled Mussels

This is a terrific hors d'oeuvre to serve at a cocktail party.

In a large stockpot, bring to a boil the water, wine, thyme, and bay leaf. Add the mussels, cover, and simmer until the mussels open, about 6 minutes.

Pour the steamed mussels into a large strainer, catching the juices in a bowl. Discard any unopened mussels.

Remove and discard the top shells of each mussel, placing the mussels in the half shell on a baking sheet.

Preheat the broiler for 15 minutes. Line 12 plates with the cabbage chiffonade.

To make the topping, combine the ingredients and sprinkle evenly over each mussel. Broil about 3 inches from the heat source until slightly browned, about 4 minutes, then divide among the 12 serving plates. Serve hot.

YIELD: 12 SERVINGS AS A FIRST COURSE.

1 cup water
2 cups dry white wine
1 sprig fresh thyme
1 bay leaf
8 dozen clean mussels
8 savoy cabbage leaves, shredded into
   a chiffonade

TOPPING

5 teaspoons minced garlic
¼ cup minced fresh parsley
8 tablespoons (1 stick) butter, softened
½ teaspoon coarse salt
1 teaspoon freshly ground black pepper
¼ cup bread crumbs
⅓ cup cooking liquid from mussels

Chicken Breasts Filled with Wild Mushrooms and Leeks

8 whole chicken breasts, bones and
    skins removed, cut in half

FILLING

2 ounces dry porcini mushrooms
1 cup hot water
4 tablespoons (½ stick) butter
2 tablespoons olive oil
5 leeks, white part only, chopped fine
Coarse salt and pepper to taste
½ teaspoon dried thyme

SAUCE

8 tablespoons (1 stick) butter, softened
4 cups chicken stock (page 8)
1½ cups white wine
2 tablespoons unbleached white flour
¼ cup port wine
¼ cup chopped fresh parsley

Cut a pocket in each half chicken breast by placing your hand flat on top and carefully slicing the chicken horizontally under your palm, being sure to slit only three-quarters of the way through. Set aside.

Soak the mushrooms in the water for 20 minutes.

Heat 4 tablespoons of the butter with the olive oil in a sauté pan. Add the leeks, salt, pepper, and thyme. Sauté until the leeks are soft, about 10 minutes. Remove from the heat and set aside.

Drain the mushrooms into a bowl, reserving the liquid. Strain this liquid through cheesecloth into another bowl and save for the sauce. Rinse the mushrooms well, and chop fine. Add them to the leek mixture, place over medium heat, and sauté for 2 minutes more. Cool slightly.

To stuff the chicken, use 1 tablespoon of the slightly cooled leek-mushroom filling per pocket. Weave a wooden toothpick through the opening of each pocket to hold the filling in place while browning the breasts. Set aside.

Heat 4 tablespoons of butter in the same sauté pan used to cook the chicken. Without crowding the pan, brown the chicken pieces on both sides, turning them carefully. When browned, transfer the chicken to a baking dish. Remove the toothpicks, cover the dish tightly with foil, and leave at room temperature.

To make the sauce, deglaze the sauté pan with the chicken stock, being sure to scrape up all the brown bits from the bottom. Add the white wine and mushroom liquid, bring to a boil, and reduce the liquid over high heat until about 3 cups remain. Knead together the flour and the remaining 4 tablespoons of butter, until it has a doughlike consistency. Add this to the sauce, a little at a time, whisking until sauce thickens. Strain the sauce into a saucepan. Add the port wine, salt and pepper to taste, and set aside.

Preheat the oven to 375 degrees. Bake the chicken for 30 minutes.

When ready to serve, reheat the sauce over medium heat.

Transfer the chicken to a serving platter. Spoon a little sauce over the meat and sprinkle with parsley. Pass the remaining sauce separately in a sauceboat.

YIELD: 12 SERVINGS.

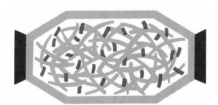

Buttered Green Beans with Nutmeg

Drop the beans into a large pot of boiling salted water. Cook for 3 minutes. The beans should still be crisp and very green. Drain, and rinse with cold water to stop the cooking process. Set the beans aside.

Ten minutes before serving, melt the butter in a large sauté pan. Add the beans, and sauté over low heat for 8 minutes, or until heated through. Toss in the nutmeg, parsley, pepper, and salt, and serve.

4 pounds green beans, ends removed
6 tablespoons butter
1½ teaspoons freshly grated nutmeg
½ cup minced fresh parsley
1 teaspoon freshly ground black pepper
1½ teaspoons coarse salt

YIELD: 12 SERVINGS.

Hot Apricot Soufflé

This magical dessert is a great favorite with our customers at Loaves and Fishes.

¾ pound dried apricots
1 cup sugar
3 tablespoons lemon juice
1½ tablespoons Grand Marnier
9 egg whites, at room temperature
Confectioners' sugar for dusting
2 cups heavy cream, whipped

Place the apricots, sugar, and 3½ cups of water in a medium saucepan. Bring to a boil. Lower the heat, and simmer for 30 minutes. Transfer the apricots to the bowl of a food processor fitted with a steel blade. Purée until smooth. Add the lemon juice and Grand Marnier. Purée 5 seconds more. Scrape the mixture into a large bowl and chill for 1 hour.

Preheat the oven to 375 degrees. Butter and sugar twelve 1-cup ramekins, a 3-quart soufflé dish, or a 3-quart shallow casserole.

Beat the egg whites until soft peaks hold. Fold them into the apricot mixture, being careful not to deflate the egg whites.

Pour the soufflé mixture into the buttered and sugared ramekins. Place the ramekins or dishes in a shallow roasting pan, and add enough hot water to reach one-third of the way up the sides of the ramekins.

Bake 25 to 30 minutes, for ramekins or 35 to 40 minutes for soufflé dish or casserole, until tops are well browned.

Dust the soufflés with confectioners' sugar, and serve with whipped cream on the side.

YIELD: 12 SERVINGS.

THANKSGIVING
FOR TWELVE

This is not the conventional recipe for either the turkey or the stuffing, but one I think you will find both mouthwatering and exciting.

If possible, use a fresh turkey. If not, allow your frozen turkey to thaw in the refrigerator. This will take about 3 days.

The Apricot-Sage Stuffing, Tomato-Clam Soup, Cranberry-Lime Chutney, and the Purée of Broccoli can all be completed the day before and stored in the refrigerator. When ready to eat, the Tomato-Clam soup can be reheated in a saucepan. The puréed broccoli should be baked in a pre-heated 350-degree oven for about 45 minutes.

The Nuss Torte and Coconut Cream Pie should be made Thanksgiving morning. The tantalizing aroma of freshly baked pies hovers in the air, and blends so well with the savory bouquet of a roasting turkey.

Prepare your salsify and carrrots no more than 2 hours ahead. If you are new to salsify, it is a sweet root vegetable very much like a carrot, with a black exterior and a white interior. It would be advisable to wear gloves when you're peeling them, since the black tends to discolor your hands. Another suggestion included in the recipe is to peel and julienne one salsify at a time, making sure you submerge it immediately in the milk so it doesn't discolor.

The mellow red of the Tomato-Clam Soup, the vivid greenness of the broccoli purée, the bright crimson cranberries, ivory salsify, yellow carrots flecked with parsley share the spotlight with the richly glazed, bountiful turkey, and make this meal not only a feast for the palate, but for your eyes as well.

TOMATO-CLAM SOUP

GARLIC-GLAZED ROAST TURKEY
APRICOT-SAGE STUFFING
CALVADOS PAN GRAVY

PURÉE OF BROCCOLI

FRESH SALSIFY AND CARROTS

CRANBERRY-LIME CHUTNEY

NUSS TORTE
COCONUT CREAM PIE

Tomato-Clam Soup

This simple and superb soup, served with a hearty bread and a salad of lacy mixed greens, can be a meal in itself.

4 tablespoons butter
2 cups finely chopped onions
4 cups clam juice
3½ pounds fresh juicy tomatoes, chopped
½ teaspoon freshly ground black pepper
½ cup heavy cream
2 tablespoons finely chopped scallions

Melt the butter in a large saucepan, add the onions, and cook over low heat for 5 minutes, making sure the onions don't brown. Add the clam juice and tomatoes. Bring to a boil, and simmer for 15 minutes.

Allow the soup to cool slightly before puréeing in a blender or food processor. Return the soup to the saucepan. Add the pepper and heavy cream. Just before serving, garnish with scallions.

YIELD: 12 SERVINGS.

Garlic-Glazed Roast Turkey
Apricot-Sage Stuffing
Calvados Pan Gravy

One 22-pound fresh turkey
5 teaspoons minced garlic
2 tablespoons coarse salt
1½ teaspoons freshly ground black pepper

Rinse the turkey and pat it dry. Place the garlic, salt, and pepper on a cutting board and make a paste, using the side of a large heavy knife. Rub the garlic paste evenly over the entire turkey. Store in the refrigerator covered with a damp towel until ready to fill.

To make the turkey stock, sauté the turkey neck and giblets with the butter in a heavy saucepan. When browned, add 7 cups cold water, the onion, carrot, and celery. Bring to a boil and simmer, covered, over low heat for 2 hours. Strain the liquid into a bowl and set aside, discarding the solids.

To make the stuffing, scatter the bread cubes onto 2 large baking sheets and toast in 375-degree oven until browned.

Melt the butter in a large sauté pan, add the onions, and sauté over a low heat for 5 minutes. Mix in the celery, apples, apricots, and pistachios. When thoroughly blended, add the sage, thyme, salt, and pepper. Toss in the toasted bread and blend thoroughly.

Fill the turkey cavities with the stuffing, making sure it is not packed too tightly. Spoon the remaining stuffing into a buttered casserole, and bake, covered, the last hour along with the turkey.

Preheat the oven to 375 degrees.

Transfer the stuffed turkey to a roasting pan. Roast 1½ hours. Remove, and pour 2½ cups of turkey stock into the pan around the turkey, and roast for another 2 hours. If the turkey browns too fast, cover loosely with foil.

Take the turkey from the oven, transfer it to a heated serving platter, cover with foil, and let it rest for 15 minutes, saving the pan scrapings and juice for the gravy.

To make the gravy, melt the butter in a heavy saucepan and, stirring constantly, add the flour. Cook 2 minutes over low heat. While stirring, add the turkey stock, wine, and Calvados. Bring to a boil and simmer for 5 minutes. Skim off any fat from the roasting pan juices, and add the juices to the gravy, along with the brown bits scraped from the bottom of the pan.

Return the gravy to a boil and, stirring occasionally, cook until the sauce starts to thicken, about 5 minutes. Strain the gravy into a warm sauceboat or pitcher.

Garnish the turkey platter with fresh sage and dried apricots.

YIELD: 12 SERVINGS

STOCK

Neck and giblets from turkey
1 tablespoon butter
½ onion, cut in half
½ carrot, cut in half
½ stalk celery, cut in half

APRICOT-SAGE STUFFING

22 slices white bread, cut into ½-inch cubes
12 tablespoons (1½ sticks) butter
3 cups chopped onions
1½ cups chopped celery
2 tart apples, cut into ½-inch pieces
12 dried apricots, chopped
½ cup chopped toasted pistachio nuts
2 tablespoons chopped fresh sage, or 1½ teaspoons dried
1 tablespoon chopped fresh thyme, or ¾ teaspoon dried
1½ teaspoons coarse salt
1 teaspoon freshly ground black pepper

CALVADOS PAN GRAVY

4 tablespoons butter
½ cup unbleached white flour
4 cups turkey stock
1 cup dry white wine
¼ cup Calvados

Fresh sage sprigs
24 dried apricots

Purée of Broccoli

If you have any leftovers, this makes a wonderful omelet filling, especially when enriched with a generous sprinkle of Parmesan cheese.

6½ pounds (4 heads) broccoli, cut into florets
8 tablespoons (1 stick) butter
1 tablespoon salt
1¼ teaspoons freshly ground black pepper
1 teaspoon grated lemon peel

Bring 2 inches of water to a boil in a large covered pot. Add the broccoli florets, and cook until tender, about 4 minutes.

Place one-third of the broccoli and butter in the bowl of a food processor fitted with a steel blade. Purée until smooth. Spoon into a buttered 12-cup casserole. Continue until all the broccoli has been puréed, adding the salt, pepper, and lemon peel to the last batch. Stir once, to make sure the purée is well blended in the casserole. Cover, and keep warm in the oven until ready to serve.

YIELD: 12 SERVINGS.

Fresh Salsify and Carrots

1 quart milk
2 pounds salsify
6 tablespoons butter
2 pounds carrots, peeled and cut into ⅛-inch rounds
½ cup chopped fresh parsley
1¼ teaspoons coarse salt
1¼ teaspoons freshly ground black pepper

Pour the milk into a medium saucepan.

Peel the salsify with a vegetable peeler. One by one, cut the salsify into a ¼-inch thick julienne, and immediately drop it into the milk so it doesn't discolor. When all the salsify has been peeled and julienned, bring the milk to a boil, lower heat, and simmer for 4 to 5 minutes. The salsify should be crisp, but tender. Drain, discarding the milk, and put the salsify back into the pan. Add the butter, cover, and leave on the stove to keep warm.

In another saucepan, cover the carrots with water and cook until tender, about 6 to 7 minutes. Drain, and add the carrots to the salsify. Sprinkle the vegetables with the parsley, salt, and pepper. Shake the saucepan to mix the ingredients.

Spoon into a warm serving bowl.

YIELD: 12 SERVINGS.

Cranberry-Lime Chutney

Sweet and tart, this is an excellent accompaniment to duck, ham, and goose, and of course, the holiday turkey.

In a saucepan, bring to a boil the lime slices, onion, garlic, sugar, brown sugar, apple cider vinegar, spices, and salt. Cover, and simmer 20 minutes. Add the apples and raisins. Return to a boil and simmer another 10 minutes. Add the cranberries and cook, covered, for 10 minutes more. Cool.

   To store the chutney, cover and refrigerate. Bring to room temperature before serving.

NOTE: Refrigerated, this chutney will keep for up to 3 months.

YIELD: 6 CUPS, 12 OR MORE SERVINGS.

1 lime, very thinly sliced
¾ cup finely chopped onions
½ teaspoon minced garlic
1 cup sugar
½ cup light brown sugar
⅔ cup apple cider vinegar
½ teaspoon ground cinnamon
⅛ teaspoon ground cloves
⅛ teaspoon ground allspice
¼ teaspoon cayenne
1 teaspoon salt
¾ cup peeled and coarsely chopped
   tart apples
½ cup dark raisins
4 cups fresh cranberries

Nuss Torte

CRUST

1 cup walnut pieces
½ cup pecans
¼ cup unbleached white flour
¼ cup sugar
6 tablespoons cold butter, cut into
   small pieces

FILLING

3 eggs
2 teaspoons vanilla extract
1 cup light corn syrup
½ cup light brown sugar
1 tablespoon Frangelica liqueur
   (optional)
½ teaspoon ground cinnamon
½ teaspoon freshly ground black
   pepper
4 tablespoons butter, melted
2 tablespoons unbleached white flour
½ teaspoon baking soda
1 cup chocolate chips
1½ cups pecan halves

2 cups heavy cream
2 tablespoons confectioners' sugar
¾ teaspoon ground cinnamon

Preheat the oven to 375 degrees. Butter a 9-inch springform pan.

To make the crust, place the walnuts, pecans, flour, and sugar in the bowl of a food processor fitted with a steel blade; process until fine, about 30 seconds. Add the butter, and pulse 6 times, until the mixture is crumbly. Gather and press into the buttered springform pan, covering the bottom and ¾ inch up the side. Set aside.

To make the filling, break the eggs into the bowl of an electric mixer. Add the vanilla, corn syrup, brown sugar, Frangelica, cinnamon, and pepper. Beat at high speed for 3 minutes. Add the butter, flour, baking soda, chocolate chips, and pecan halves. Beat at low speed just to combine.

Pour the filling into the nut pastry shell. Smooth the top and bake for 45 minutes.

When the pie is done, allow it to cool for 10 minutes, then transfer it to a flat cake plate.

When ready to serve, whip together the heavy cream, confectioners' sugar, and cinnamon until the beater leaves light ribbons on the surface of the cream.

Serve the pie warm, with the cream passed separately.

YIELD: 12 SERVINGS.

Coconut Cream Pie

Place the flour in the bowl of a food processor fitted with a steel blade. Add the butter, and pulse 5 times. Add the lemon juice and cold water. Process 5 seconds. Scrape the mixture onto a countertop. Gather it into a ball, and chill, covered in plastic wrap, about 30 minutes.

Preheat the oven to 375 degrees.

On a lightly floured surface, roll the dough into a 12-inch circle. Fit it into a 10-inch pie plate. Cut off the excess dough, and flute the edges. Prick the pastry several times with a fork. Cover with foil and fill with beans. Bake for 15 minutes. Remove the beans and foil. Bake 5 minutes more. Remove from the oven, and set aside to cool.

To make the filling, combine the sugar, cornstarch, and milk in a heavy saucepan. Mix well. Bring to a boil, stirring constantly. Simmer for 2 minutes. Remove from the heat, add the butter and egg yolks, and beat vigorously with a whisk. Blend in the coconut and vanilla seeds, stirring well. Pour the filling into the baked pie shell, cover with plastic wrap, and chill.

Shortly before serving, whip together the heavy cream, confectioners' sugar, and vanilla seeds, until soft peaks hold. Fold in the sour cream and coconut. Spread the topping over the pie. Refrigerate, uncovered, until ready to serve.

YIELD: 12 SERVINGS.

CRUST

1½ cups unbleached white flour
¼ pound (1 stick) cold butter, cut into small pieces
1 tablespoon lemon juice
3½ tablespoons cold water

FILLING

¼ cup granulated sugar
3 tablespoons cornstarch
2 cups milk
2 tablespoons butter
4 egg yolks
1 cup flaked sweetened coconut
Seeds of half a vanilla bean

TOPPING

½ cup heavy cream
½ cup confectioners' sugar
Seeds of half a vanilla bean
½ cup sour cream
½ cup flaked coconut

SUNDAY AFTERNOON TEA
FOR TEN TO TWELVE

**DANISH OPEN-FACED
SANDWICHES
(SMORREBROD):**

SARDINE, EGG, AND
GREEN PEPPER SANDWICHES

CHEESE, PEAR, AND
SPROUT SANDWICHES

OATMEAL-ORANGE SCONES
WITH BUTTER AND JAM

LEMON COOKIES

MOIST CHOCOLATE COOKIES

This particular menu comes from my mother's own kitchen, and is one that I remember with special fondness. It includes a refreshing balance of savory and sweet, hot and cold, with nothing too heavy yet everything vastly gratifying.

Many of the foods are simple to prepare, leaving you time to enjoy the afternoon with your guests.

Since the Lemon Cookie mixture has to be chilled for at least 6 hours, and the Moist Chocolate Cookie mix needs to sit overnight in the refrigerator, it would be wise to prepare these the day before and bake them the morning of the tea.

The spreads are very easy to make and can be prepared in the morning and refrigerated. You can assemble the sandwiches an hour before your guests arrive and cover the platter with a slightly dampened tea towel to keep them moist until ready to serve.

The scones should be made not longer than 1 hour before serving time. They should be served warm, with the butter and jam on the side. And think of the marvelous aroma that will filter out to greet your friends!

Sardine, Egg, and Green Pepper Sandwiches

Combine the sardines, ¼ cup sardine oil, onion, green pepper, egg, lemon peel, lemon juice, pepper, and salt on a large plate and mash with a fork until the mixture holds together while still retaining some texture.

Spread the mixture evenly over the seven slices of bread. Cut each slice into four pieces and sprinkle with chopped parsley.

Arrange the open-faced sandwiches on a platter, garnish with lemon wedges, and serve at room temperature.

YIELD: 28 SANDWICHES.

Two 4½-ounce cans skinless and
    boneless sardines, drained (reserving
    ¼ cup of the oil for the spread)
1 tablespoon minced onion
¼ cup minced green bell pepper
1 hard-boiled egg, minced
3 tablespoons lemon juice
1½ teaspoons grated lemon peel
¾ teaspoon freshly ground black
    pepper
½ teaspoon coarse salt
7 slices dark whole-grain bread
¼ cup minced fresh parsley
12 lemon wedges

Cheese, Pear, and Sprout Sandwiches

Using a fork, lightly mash the cheese on a large plate. Add the pear, ½ cup of alfalfa sprouts, the olive oil, pepper, and salt. Mash until the ingredients cling together, but still have some texture.

Spread the mixture evenly over the 24 slices of bread. Garnish with the remaining alfalfa sprouts.

YIELD: 24 SANDWICHES.

6 ounces fresh goat cheese, such as
    Montrachet
1 ripe pear, peeled, cored, and minced
1 cup alfalfa sprouts
⅓ cup olive oil
1 teaspoon freshly ground black pepper
½ teaspoon coarse salt
24 thin slices French bread

Oatmeal-Orange Scones

3 cups unbleached white flour
1½ cups old-fashioned oats
2 tablespoons baking powder
1 teaspoon baking soda
1 teaspoon salt
⅓ cup light brown sugar
½ pound (2 sticks) cold butter, cut into small pieces
3 eggs
2 tablespoons grated orange peel
⅓ cup orange juice
½ cup sour cream
½ cup chopped walnuts
1 egg yolk
1 tablespoon milk

Preheat the oven to 400 degrees.

Place the flour, oats, baking powder, baking soda, salt, brown sugar, and butter in the bowl of an electric mixer. Mix at low speed for 15 seconds. Add the eggs and the orange peel. Mix at low speed for 5 seconds. Add the orange juice, sour cream, and walnuts; mix just to blend, about 5 seconds. Scrape the mixture onto a floured countertop and flatten it with your hands to a 1-inch thickness. Cut as many scones as you can with a 2-inch biscuit cutter. Gather the remaining dough and pat to a 1-inch thickness. Cut more scones.

Place the scones 1 inch apart on a buttered baking sheet. Mix the egg yolk with the milk, and brush the scones with the egg wash. Bake 15 to 17 minutes, or until golden brown.

Serve warm, with room-temperature butter and your favorite jam.

YIELD: APPROXIMATELY 15 SCONES.

Lemon Cookies

8 tablespoons (1 stick) butter, at room temperature
1 cup sugar
1 egg
2½ teaspoons grated lemon peel
1½ tablespoons lemon juice
2½ cups unbleached white flour
1 teaspoon baking powder
¼ teaspoon salt

Combine the butter and sugar in the bowl of an electric mixer, and cream until light and fluffy. Add the egg, lemon peel, and lemon juice. Mix to blend. Add the flour, baking powder, and salt; mix until combined, about 2 minutes.

Turn the dough out onto a lightly floured countertop. Form it into a 12-inch-long roll. Cover with plastic wrap and refrigerate at least 6 hours before baking.

Preheat the oven to 400 degrees.

Cut the rolls into ¼-inch slices. Place them on a buttered cookie sheet and bake 10 to 12 minutes, or until the edges start to brown slightly. Transfer the cookies to a countertop to cool.

YIELD: 48 COOKIES.

Moist Chocolate Cookies

I find myself making these cookies quite frequently throughout the year, both for my customers and my husband. The mixture needs to be chilled in a covered bowl for at least 6 hours or overnight.

Preheat the oven to 250 degrees.

Place the chocolate in a pie plate and melt it in the pre-heated oven. Transfer the warm chocolate to the bowl of an electric mixer. Add the safflower oil, sugar, and vanilla; mix at low speed for 1 minute. Add the eggs, flour, and baking powder. Mix to blend well.

Chill the batter for at least 6 hours in the refrigerator.

Preheat the oven to 300 degrees.

Scoop out a teaspoon of dough. Roll it into a ball. Roll the ball in confectioners' sugar, coating it well before placing it on a lightly buttered baking sheet. Continue with the rest of the batter, placing the balls about 2 inches apart.

Bake for 10 minutes. Do not overbake.

Transfer the cookies to a countertop. After they cool, store them in an airtight container. They will stay moist for about 2 days.

4 ounces unsweetened chocolate

½ cup safflower oil

2¼ cups granulated sugar

1 tablespoon vanilla extract

4 eggs

2 cups unbleached white flour

2 teaspoons baking powder

1½ cups confectioners' sugar

YIELD: 80 COOKIES.

THE GLOW OF WINTER

FAMILY GATHERING FOR TWENTY-FOUR

HOLIDAY BUFFET FOR THIRTY

WINTER WEDDING RECEPTION FOR THIRTY

A COUNTRY LUNCH FOR EIGHT

CHRISTMAS EVE SUPPER FOR EIGHT

A DANISH CHRISTMAS BREAKFAST FOR EIGHT

CHRISTMAS DINNER FOR EIGHT

NEW YEAR'S EVE DINNER FOR TWELVE

NEW YEAR'S DAY OPEN HOUSE FOR THIRTY

APRÈS SKATING SUPPER FOR TWELVE

Before I began assembling this section of the book, I thought back to a trip my husband, Detlef, and I made one winter when I was invited to cook at the American embassy in Vienna. We arrived late in October and stayed for five thrilling weeks, during which time I scoured every marketplace in Vienna, looking for the freshest produce, fish, poultry, and meats the city had to offer. The best, I thought, was the Nasch Markt, a glorious outdoor market that went on for almost a mile and displayed the most spectacular and varied selection of foods I have ever seen. With this reservoir as my inspiration, I quickly reacquainted myself with the delights of Viennese cuisine; fresh game roasted to a mahogany crispness, goose and pheasant infused with aromatic herbs, sausages bursting with flavor, dark and rich rye breads, nut dumplings that complement any stew or casserole, cakes spiked with liqueurs and gentled with dollops of fresh cream, pastries so light and flaky they melt in your mouth. Cooking these delights was quite a challenge and a memorable experience. When we returned home I noticed that my recipe file had doubled in bulk.

Even though I have peppered this section with many of the recipes I developed and discovered in Vienna, there are also some dishes that come from my mother's Danish kitchen and others that are strictly innovations of Loaves and Fishes. In other words, a mingling of the old with the new.

FAMILY GATHERING
FOR TWENTY-FOUR

RAW CLAMS AND
OYSTERS WITH
SPICY HORSERADISH SAUCE

SAUSAGES

ROAST TURKEY BREAST
WITH PECAN AND
WILD RICE FILLING

BEET, CARROT, AND
ENDIVE SALAD

BAKED KALE, LEEK,
AND POTATOES

DARK RYE BREAD

APPLE STRUDEL

KIRSCH TORTE

Inspired by my trip to Vienna, I improvised the following menu for a customer's thirty-fifth wedding anniversary. The meal is substantial and hearty, yet with overtones of European elegance. It's a perfect menu for any festive occasion, and with a little planning it is quite simple to prepare.

The Dark Rye Bread, for instance, can be made up to 1 week before the dinner, when wrapped and stored in your freezer.

Make the Kirsch Torte sponge 2 days ahead. If it's wrapped well, it will keep in your refrigerator until the day of the party. Finish it 2 hours before serving time.

The Spicy Horseradish Sauce can be made 4 days ahead and kept refrigerated until the day of the gathering.

I would prepare the kale casserole the day before the party, and bake it just before serving time.

The Apple Strudel should be made the day of the event, since it is best when served warm and freshly baked.

My favorite sausages are boudin noir, or blutwurst (blood sausages). They have a robust flavor, and a coarse, country texture. I also suggest bockwurst (veal sausages), which are gently flavored with chive and terrifically tasty when broiled, poached, grilled, or sautéed. Italian link sausages, hot or sweet, sometimes flavored with a hint of anise, are marvelous, too.

The clams and oysters should be bought fresh the morning of the gathering and, I suggest, opened by your fishmonger. No other appetizer can compare with these cool, delectable treats; the perfect starter for a well-rounded meal that is crowned by two very special desserts.

Raw Clams and Oysters with Spicy Horseradish Sauce

This Spicy Horseradish Sauce also goes extremely well with poached or steamed shrimp.

To make the sauce, sauté the onions in the olive oil over medium heat for about 5 minutes. Add the garlic, tomatoes, cayenne, salt, and bay leaf. Bring to a boil, then simmer, covered, for 20 minutes. Cool. Remove and discard the bay leaf.

Purée the sauce in a food processor until smooth. Add the horseradish, and pulse to blend.

When ready to serve, insert toothpicks in the center of each clam and oyster, and arrange on a large serving platter covered with crushed ice. Place the Spicy Horseradish Sauce in a small bowl in the center, and garnish with lemon wedges and sprigs of fresh parsley.

YIELD: 3 CUPS SPICY HORSERADISH SAUCE, 24 SERVINGS.

SPICY HORSERADISH SAUCE

2 cups chopped onions
¼ cup olive oil
2 teaspoons minced garlic
3 cups plum tomatoes with their juices
   (fresh or canned)
¼ teaspoon cayenne
1 teaspoon salt
1 bay leaf
1 cup freshly grated horseradish, or
   ½ cup prepared

4 dozen fresh clams, opened on the half
   shell, on ice
4 dozen fresh oysters, opened on the
   half shell, on ice
24 lemon wedges
1 bunch fresh parsley sprigs

Sausages

I have suggested my favorite sausages in the introduction to this menu. Broiled, grilled, or sautéed, these sausages look wonderful arranged on a large wooden serving tray, decorated with parsley and watercress sprigs. If you choose Italian sausages and have any leftovers, crumble or slice the pieces and add them to scrambled eggs. This is a perfect breakfast or brunch with warm, flaky croissants, slathered with sweet butter.

YIELD: 24 SERVINGS, 2 SAUSAGES PER PERSON.

48 sausages, such as boudin noir or
   blutwurst, bockwurst, Italian hot or
   sweet
Parsley and watercress sprigs for
   garnishing

Roast Turkey Breast with Pecan and Wild Rice Filling

FILLING

¼ pound (1 stick) butter

4 cups coarsely chopped onions

2 tablespoons minced garlic

4 cups wild rice

2 teaspoons coarse salt

2 teaspoons freshly ground black pepper

9 cups chicken stock (page 8)

1½ cups (6 ounces) coarsely chopped pecans

Two 8-pound fresh, whole turkey breasts, bones and skin intact

Coarse salt and freshly ground black pepper

1 cup white wine

Fresh parsley sprigs

To make the filling, melt the butter in a heavy saucepan. Add the onions, and sauté for 5 minutes. Add the garlic and sauté for another 2 minutes. Add the rice, salt, pepper, and chicken stock. Cover, bring to a boil, and simmer for 30 minutes, or until the rice is al dente.

In a large skillet, toss the pecans gently over medium heat until lightly browned. Set aside.

Remove the filling from the heat, and fold in the toasted pecans.

Preheat the oven to 350 degrees.

Remove the turkey bones, taking care not to break the skin. Place the breasts, skin side down, on a countertop. Sprinkle with salt and pepper. Spoon one-quarter of the filling, lengthwise, down the center of each turkey breast. Fold the skin and side flaps over the stuffing to create a roll. Tie string around the roll, securing each turkey breast in three places. Transfer the remaining half of the filling to a small ovenproof casserole, and set aside.

Place the stuffed turkey breasts in a roasting pan. Sprinkle with salt and pepper. Roast, uncovered, for 1 hour. Add the wine, cover the breasts with foil, and roast 1 more hour.

The remaining stuffing in the casserole should be placed in the oven for the last 45 minutes of the turkey's roasting time.

Remove from the oven, leave roll covered with foil, and let the meat rest for 15 minutes. Remove the string, and cut the turkey into ¼-inch slices.

To serve, spoon the stuffing from the casserole onto a large serving platter. Arrange the turkey slices on top. Garnish with fresh parsley sprigs.

YIELD: 24 SERVINGS.

Beet, Carrot, and Endive Salad

Crisp, crunchy, and refreshing, this salad also lends bright colors to the meal.

Grate the beets and carrots, either by hand or in a food processor. Transfer the grated vegetables to a large salad bowl. Peel and slice the onion into thin, half-moon rings, and cut the endive lengthwise into thin strips. Add to the salad.

To make the dressing, place the ingredients in the bowl of a food processor. Process until smooth, about 15 seconds. Dress the salad just before serving.

YIELD: 24 SERVINGS.

8 medium beets, peeled
12 medium carrots, peeled
1 small red onion
2 heads endive

DRESSING

1 egg yolk
¾ cup extra-virgin olive oil
3 tablespoons red wine vinegar
1 tablespoon Dijon mustard
1 tablespoon heavy cream
½ teaspoon cayenne
2 teaspoons salt

Baked Kale, Leek, and Potatoes

This is a wonderfully hearty dish for the winter months, and the perfect accompaniment for any poultry or meat.

1 pound bacon, cut into bite-size pieces

8 leeks, cut into ½-inch-thick rings

6½ pounds fresh kale, blanched and finely chopped, or ten 10-ounce packages frozen chopped kale

5½ pounds baking potatoes, peeled and cut into quarters

½ pound (2 sticks) butter, melted

1½ cups heavy cream

1½ cups chicken stock

1½ tablespoons coarse salt

1 tablespoon freshly ground black pepper

Fry the bacon in a large, heavy sauté pan until crisp. Transfer the bacon to a small bowl, and set aside. Discard all but 3 tablespoons of bacon fat from the pan. Add the leeks to the sauté pan, and over medium heat, sauté, covered, for 15 minutes, stirring occasionally to make sure they don't brown. Add the kale (if using frozen kale, press out all the water before adding to the leeks), and sauté for 5 minutes.

Preheat the oven to 350 degrees.

While the vegetables are cooking, boil the potatoes in salted water until tender. Drain, and add them to the kale-leek mixture.

Add 12 tablespoons of melted butter, the heavy cream, chicken stock, salt, and pepper to the vegetables.

Using the potato masher, coarsely purée the mixture. Spoon into a buttered 5-quart casserole with 2- to 2½-inch sides. Dot the vegetables with the remaining 4 tablespoons of butter, and sprinkle with the crisp bacon pieces.

Cover with foil, and bake 30 minutes.

Transfer to a large serving platter, and serve warm.

YIELD: 24 SERVINGS.

Dark Rye Bread

Combine the yeast, warm water, and molasses in a large mixing bowl. Set aside for 5 minutes, until the yeast begins to bubble.

Add the rye flour, salt, cardamom, and olive oil. Stir hard for 8 to 10 minutes. Mix in the raisins and the white flour until combined.

Turn the dough onto a flour-dusted countertop. Knead for 5 minutes, or until the dough is smooth and elastic. Return to the bowl, cover with a kitchen towel, and let rise in a warm place for 2 hours, or until it has doubled in bulk.

Divide the dough into 3 equal pieces. Shape each piece into a ball, then place all 3 loaves on a flour-dusted baking sheet. In a small bowl, mix the egg yolks with the heavy cream, and brush the loaves with the egg wash. Let rise until doubled, about 1 hour.

Preheat the oven to 350 degrees. Bake the loaves for 40 minutes. Cool on a wire rack. Cut each loaf into 10 slices.

6 tablespoons active dry yeast
3 cups warm water
1 cup dark molasses
5 cups rye flour
2 tablespoons salt
1 tablespoon ground cardamom
½ cup olive oil
1½ cups raisins
5 cups unbleached white flour
1 egg yolk
1 tablespoon heavy cream

YIELD: 3 LOAVES, 30 SLICES.

Apple Strudel

PASTRY

4 cups unbleached white flour

2 tablespoons sugar

½ teaspoon salt

½ pound (2 sticks) cold margarine, cut into 16 pieces

¼ pound (1 stick) cold butter, cut into 8 pieces

1 egg yolk

12 tablespoons cold water

FILLING

12 cups peeled and thinly sliced apples, preferably Granny Smith

4 tablespoons lime juice

2 teaspoons ground cinnamon

⅓ cup sugar

2 tablespoons unbleached white flour

1 cup raisins

1 cup walnut pieces

4 tablespoons butter, melted

⅓ cup confectioners' sugar

To make the pastry, place the flour, sugar, salt, margarine, and butter in the large bowl of a food processor fitted with a steel blade. Pulse 5 times, or until the butter is the size of small peas. Add the egg yolk, and 12 tablespoons of cold water. Process until the mixture forms a ball. Depending on the size of your food processor, you may want to do this in 2 batches. Cover the dough in plastic wrap, and chill for 30 minutes.

To make the filling, combine all the ingredients in a mixing bowl, and toss to blend.

Preheat the oven to 450 degrees. Butter two 12 x 17-inch baking sheets.

Divide the dough in half. On a piece of cheesecloth dusted with flour, roll one half of the dough into a 14 x 16-inch rectangle. Ladle half the apple filling evenly over the dough. Lift the cheesecloth from one end, and roll up the dough, jelly-roll fashion. Press the edges together to seal the ends. Repeat this process with the remaining dough and filling to create a second strudel.

Gently slide the strudels onto the prepared baking sheets. Brush with the melted butter, and bake 35 to 40 minutes, or until the strudels are golden brown and the apples feel tender when pierced with a sharp knife. Cool.

When ready to serve, dust the strudels with confectioners' sugar, and lift them onto a flat plate or cutting board. Cut each strudel into 12 even pieces.

YIELD: 2 STRUDELS, 24 SERVINGS.

Kirsch Torte

A traditional dessert at winter festivities, this torte is very rich, and one cake, along with the two strudels, should be ample indulgence for 24 guests.

Preheat the oven to 350 degrees. Butter the bottom of a 9½-inch springform pan.

Using the whisk attachment to an electric mixer, beat together the eggs, sugar, and half the seeds from the vanilla bean. Whip until tripled in volume, about 10 minutes.

Sift together the cocoa powder, flour, and baking powder.

Fold the dry ingredients into the egg mixture by hand. Pour the batter into the prepared pan, and smooth the top.

Bake for 35 minutes, without opening the oven door. Remove from the oven, and run a knife around the edge to loosen the cake from the pan. As it cools, the cake will shrink slightly.

When the cake is completely cool, spread a sheet of wax paper on the countertop, and transfer the cake to the paper. Carefully slice the cake, horizontally, into 3 layers. Sprinkle each layer with some of the Kirsch.

Whip the heavy cream with the confectioners' sugar and remaining vanilla bean seeds, until firm peaks hold. Transfer the bottom layer of the cake to a cake plate, spread with a little cream, and top with one-third of the cherries. Cover with the second layer and repeat the procedure. Add the final layer and, using the remaining cream, slather the top and sides of the cake. Garnish with the remaining cherries. Refrigerate until ready to serve.

NOTE: Covered, leftovers will keep in the refrigerator for 2 days.

6 eggs, at room temperature
1 cup superfine sugar
1 soft vanilla bean
½ cup unsweetened cocoa powder
½ cup unbleached white flour
1 teaspoon baking powder
¼ cup Kirschwasser
4 cups heavy cream
⅓ cup confectioners' sugar
4 cups fresh or frozen pitted black cherries

YIELD: 24 SMALL SERVINGS.

HOLIDAY BUFFET
FOR THIRTY

APPLE-GLAZED COUNTRY HAM

BAKED SALMON WITH
SZECHUAN PEPPER

POTATO AND
BLACK BEAN SALAD

CELERIAC SALAD

BAKED PEARS WITH
GOAT CHEESE FILLING

CHOCOLATE CHUNK–ORANGE
CAKE

BITTERSWEET LEMON TART

Winter seems to me to be the perfect season for ham. An economical meat, ham stretches from one meal into two or three. Whether accompanying scrambled eggs in the morning, added to a frittata for lunch, or enjoyed as a late night snack, thinly sliced on black bread with a dab of hot, grainy mustard, it makes perfect holiday fare.

An aged country ham is dry-cured with salt and pepper, often lightly smoked, and hung in an airy shed for 6 months to 1 year. The longer the ham ages, the saltier it will be. Most butchers clean their hams before selling them; however, if you spot some surface mold, don't be alarmed. Hold the ham under warm running water, and scrub away the mold with a vegetable brush.

The salad and desserts can be prepared 1 day in advance of the party and kept refrigerated. The pears, too, can be baked and stuffed, covered, and refrigerated 1 day ahead. They will only need 10 minutes of baking time in a preheated oven to take the chill off and melt the cheese.

Prepare the ham and salmon the day of the party. Their mingling aromas will offer a stimulating welcome for your friends and family.

Apple-Glazed Country Ham

This is a traditional dish, served by my mother, and adapted to include apples, which are so plentiful this time of year.

Preheat the oven to 350 degrees.

Wash the ham under running lukewarm water, using a vegetable brush to scrape away any mold. Place the ham in a large roasting pan, and pour the apple cider around it. Cover the ham with a double layer of foil, sealing tightly.

Bake for 2½ hours. Discard the foil and pour out the apple cider.

Raise the oven temperature to 375 degrees.

Melt the apple jelly in a small saucepan over low heat. Add the sugar, mustard, soy sauce, and rice vinegar. Cook until the sugar dissolves.

Remove the ham from the oven and cut away all the skin and fat you can, then hatch the top in a crisscross pattern. Coat the ham with half of the glaze. Return to the oven, uncovered, and bake for 25 minutes.

Add the apples to the roasting pan and brush the ham with the remaining apple glaze. Bake 25 minutes more.

Let the ham cool to room temperature before slicing thinly. Serve on a bed of watercress, surrounded by apple wedges.

YIELD: 35 SERVINGS.

One 14-pound fully cooked Virginia ham, bone in
2 quarts apple cider
One 10-ounce jar apple jelly
1¼ cups dark brown sugar
½ cup Dijon mustard
1 tablespoon soy sauce
1 tablespoon rice vinegar
4 Granny Smith apples, quartered and cored
3 bunches watercress, trimmed

Baked Salmon with Szechuan Pepper

One 8 to 9-pound whole fresh salmon, filleted, skin left on

¼ cup dark brown sugar

½ cup finely chopped fresh gingerroot

2 teaspoons minced garlic

1 cup finely chopped red onions

½ cup Szechuan peppercorns

1¼ cups rice wine vinegar

1 cup sesame oil

1 cup soy sauce

½ cup dry sherry

1 seedless cucumber, thinly sliced

3 lemons, thinly sliced

Preheat the oven to 400 degrees.

Place the salmon fillets, skin side down, in a nonreactive roasting pan. In the bowl of a food processor fitted with a steel blade, process the sugar, gingerroot, garlic, onions, and ¼ cup of Szechuan peppercorns for 10 seconds. Add the rice vinegar, sesame oil, soy sauce, and sherry. Process just to blend. Pour the mixture over the salmon.

Bake the fish, uncovered, for about 20 minutes, or until just done.

Serve the salmon at room temperature on two large platters. Garnish with the remaining Szechuan peppercorns, cucumber slices, and lemons.

YIELD: 30 SERVINGS.

Potato and Black Bean Salad

1 pound black turtle beans

6 pounds small new potatoes

1½ cups finely chopped onions

1½ cups chopped celery

1 cup finely chopped cornichons

1 tablespoon coarse salt

2 teaspoons freshly ground black pepper

1½ cups coarsely chopped fresh coriander

¼ cup red wine vinegar

1 cup extra-virgin olive oil

1 tablespoon Dijon mustard

6 hard-boiled eggs, peeled and sliced

Using a large pot, cook the black beans in 3 quarts of water for 50 to 60 minutes, or until the beans are tender. Drain.

Cook the potatoes, covered with boiling water, for about 15 minutes. Drain. Cut the potatoes into bite-size pieces, and place them in a large mixing bowl. Add the beans, onions, celery, cornichons, salt, pepper, and 1 cup of the coriander.

Place the wine vinegar, olive oil, and mustard in a container with a screw-top lid, and shake vigorously to mix. Pour the dressing over the salad. Toss to blend.

Transfer the salad to a serving bowl. Garnish with the egg slices and remaining coriander. Serve warm.

YIELD: 30 SERVINGS.

Celeriac Salad

Celeriac is a crunchy root vegetable that has a distinct yet subtle flavor when served raw, and a powerful taste when cooked. This salad goes very well with zesty meat and poultry dishes.

Grate the celeriac knobs by hand or in a food processor, using the shredding disk. Transfer to a mixing bowl, and add the scallions.

Whisk together the remaining ingredients, using only half of the parsley, and pour over the celeriac salad. Toss to blend well.

Sprinkle with the remaining chopped parsley, and serve at room temperature.

YIELD: 30 TO 35 SERVINGS.

5 medium celeriac knobs, peeled
2 bunches scallions, chopped
2½ cups crème fraîche (page 9)
1½ cups heavy cream
½ cup lemon juice
¼ cup Dijon mustard
1 tablespoon salt
2 teaspoons freshly ground black pepper
1 cup finely chopped fresh parsley

Baked Pears with Goat Cheese Filling

The blend of fruit, cheese, nuts, and herbs makes this a surprising and scrumptious treat. You can also spoon some Goat Cheese Filling onto thin apple slices or crisp endive leaves, and instantly you have a tray of enticing hors d'oeuvres.

1 cup walnut pieces

15 small pears, halved and cored

2 cups dry white wine

1 cup sugar

2 tablespoons olive oil

1½ cups finely chopped onions

2 teaspoons minced garlic

¼ teaspoon cayenne

8 ounces fresh goat cheese, at room temperature

8 ounces cream cheese, at room temperature

1 tablespoon lime juice

3 tablespoons walnut oil

½ cup heavy cream

¾ cup finely chopped fresh herbs, such as mint, basil, or thyme

Preheat the oven to 375 degrees.

Place the walnuts in a skillet, and stir constantly over medium heat until they start to brown. Remove from the heat and set aside.

Place the pears, cut side down, in a large nonaluminum roasting pan. Heat the wine and sugar in a medium saucepan until the sugar dissolves. Pour the liquid over the pears. Cover the roasting pan with foil and bake 20 to 25 minutes, or until the pears are tender when pierced with a knife.

Sauté the onions in the olive oil until they are transparent. Add the garlic, and sauté a few minutes more.

Transfer the onion mixture to a food processor fitted with a steel blade. Add the cayenne, goat cheese, cream cheese, lime juice, walnut oil, and heavy cream. Process until combined, about 10 seconds. Add the toasted walnuts and ¼ cup of the herbs. Pulse 3 times.

Divide the cheese mixture evenly among the pears, spooning it into the cavities and piling it high.

Place the pears, cheese side up, on a baking sheet. Cover, and store in the refrigerator for up to 24 hours.

Just before serving, bake the pears for 10 minutes in an oven preheated to 375 degrees. Transfer to a large serving platter and sprinkle with the remaining herbs. Serve slightly warm, or at room temperature.

YIELD: 30 SERVINGS.

Chocolate Chunk–Orange Cake

This extraordinary cake should be made 24 hours before serving time to give the flavors a chance to blend.

Preheat the oven to 350 degrees. Butter a 10-inch Bundt pan, or a 10-inch tube pan.

Cream the butter and sugar in the bowl of an electric mixer until light and fluffy. Blend in the eggs, two at a time. Add the orange peel, 2 cups of flour, baking powder, and sour cream. Beat to combine. Add the remaining flour and chocolate chunks. Beat at low speed until no traces of flour remain.

Spoon the batter into the buttered pan. Bake for 1 hour and 15 minutes, or until a toothpick inserted in the center comes out clean. Cool 5 minutes.

Combine the glaze ingredients in a small saucepan and heat until the sugar dissolves. Pour over the cake. Let the cake rest for 15 minutes before unmolding it onto a serving plate.

YIELD: 30 THIN SLICES.

½ pound (2 sticks) butter, softened
2½ cups sugar
6 eggs
1 tablespoon grated orange peel
3 cups unbleached white flour
1 teaspoon baking powder
1 cup sour cream
8 ounces semisweet chocolate, cut into chunks

GLAZE

1 cup orange juice
¼ cup lemon juice
¾ cup sugar

Bittersweet Lemon Tart

This recipe should not be tripled. Make three tarts, one at a time, up to three days before serving. It's well worth the effort!

PASTRY

1¼ cups unbleached white flour
¼ pound (1 stick) cold butter, cut into
    8 pieces
3 tablespoons cold water

FILLING

2 lemons
1 cup sugar
6 tablespoons very soft butter
3 eggs
⅓ cup crème fraîche (page 9)

To make the pastry crust, place the flour and butter in the bowl of a food processor fitted with a steel blade. Pulse 5 times. Add cold water, and process until the dough forms a ball. Wrap in plastic, and chill for 30 minutes.

Preheat the oven to 400 degrees.

Roll the dough into a 12-inch circle, ⅛ inch thick. Fit it into the bottom and 1 inch up the sides of a buttered, 9½-inch springform pan. Cover with foil, and fill with beans and bake for 15 minutes. Remove the beans and foil, and bake 5 minutes more.

Reduce the oven temperature to 375 degrees.

Peel the lemons with a vegetable peeler. Cut the peel into 1-inch pieces and place in the bowl of a food processor. Add the sugar and process until fine. Peel off and discard the white pith from the lemons. Cut the fruit into chunks, add to the sugar mixture in the food processor, and process for 20 seconds. Add the soft butter, eggs, and crème fraîche. Process for 10 more seconds to blend all the ingredients.

Pour the mixture into the baked crust and bake for 20 to 30 minutes, or until the custard is set. Cool to room temperature, then chill overnight.

YIELD: 10 SERVINGS (3 TARTS YIELD 30 SERVINGS).

WINTER WEDDING RECEPTION
FOR THIRTY

W e created this menu for a mature couple who wanted to follow their marriage ceremony with a reception that was both innovative and economical. It was a lively, happy affair that permitted the couple time to marry, visit with their friends, and still make a plane that evening for the Bahamas. A few days later, we received a call from one of the guests at the wedding who asked if we could prepare the same menu for her daughter's engagement party. A week later another call came from a guest who attended the engagement party, asking for precisely that menu for his son's graduation. The only alteration was the decoration on the cake. Although we refer to this meal as a Winter Wedding Reception, it can be easily adapted to fit almost any festive occasion.

Three days before the reception, bake the chocolate cakes and store them in their pans, covered, in the refrigerator.

Two days before the event, prepare the sauce for the shrimp, and bake the Apricot Bread and the Gingersnaps.

The day before, make the liver spread, prepare the Brussels sprouts, carrots, and process the niçoise mayonnaise. You can also bake the Apple-Onion Tart, but it's best to wait to add the Roquefort cheese until just before reheating. This is also the day to cut and assemble the cake, and spread the chocolate–Grand Marnier sauce between the layers.

The day of the wedding, frost the cake and decorate it with flowers. Peel and slice the oranges, sprinkle them with Grand Marnier, and serve them at room temperature with the cake.

Simple, glorious, delicious, and memorable.

CHAMPAGNE

WARM LIVER CROSTINI

SHRIMP WITH
ROASTED PEPPER
AND CAPER SAUCE

APRICOT BREAD WITH
GOAT CHEESE SPREAD

BRUSSELS SPROUTS AND
CARROTS WITH
NIÇOISE MAYONNAISE

APPLE-ONION TART

GINGERSNAPS

CHOCOLATE WEDDING CAKE

SLICED ORANGES WITH
GRAND MARNIER

Warm Liver Crostini

Crusty grilled French bread topped with a rich, meaty treat. This is an excellent hors d'oeuvre that takes less than an hour to make.

½ pound (2 sticks) butter

1½ cups finely chopped onions

2 pounds chicken livers

1 tablespoon coarse salt

1½ teaspoons freshly ground black pepper

1 cup extra-virgin olive oil

4 loaves thick French bread, cut into 80 slices

½ cup finely chopped fresh parsley

Heat the butter in a large skillet. Add the onions and chicken livers, and sauté for approximately 8 minutes, over medium-high heat, until the onions are browned and the livers are just done. Stir in the salt and pepper, and remove from the heat. When the mixture has cooled to room temperature, scrape the onions and livers into the bowl of a food processor fitted with a steel blade, and process slightly, until combined but with a coarse texture. If you plan on completing this dish later, cover the liver mixture and store in the refrigerator.

Preheat the broiler.

Brush each slice of bread with a little olive oil. Place on a baking sheet, and broil 4 inches from the heat source, until the edges are light brown.

Preheat the oven to 350 degrees.

Just before serving, spread each crostini with liver. Bake 10 minutes, sprinkle with parsley, and serve hot.

YIELD: 30 SERVINGS.

Shrimp with Roasted Pepper and Caper Sauce

Preheat the oven to 400 degrees.

Brush the bottom of a roasting pan with a little of the olive oil. Add the peppers and onions, arranging them in a single layer. Drizzle the vegetables with the remaining olive oil and the hazelnut oil. Sprinkle with the salt, and roast for 15 minutes. Sprinkle with the garlic, and roast 15 minutes longer, or until the vegetables are soft.

Transfer the contents of the roasting pan to the bowl of a food processor fitted with a steel blade. Add the wine vinegar, anchovies, capers, and pepper, and process until smooth. Chill until ready to serve.

To serve, pour the sauce into a small bowl and place it in the center of a large serving platter. Arrange the shrimp around the bowl, and garnish with lemon slices.

YIELD: 30 SERVINGS, ABOUT 8 SHRIMP PER PERSON.

½ cup olive oil

2 red bell peppers, seeded and quartered

2 medium red onions, cut into 8 pieces

¼ cup hazelnut oil

1 teaspoon coarse salt

4 cloves garlic, mashed

1 tablespoon red wine vinegar

3 flat anchovies, halved

1 tablespoon capers, drained

¾ teaspoon freshly ground black pepper

8 pounds medium shrimp, cooked, peeled, and deveined

2 lemons, thinly sliced

Apricot Bread with Goat Cheese Spread

APRICOT BREAD

¾ pound (3 sticks) butter, softened

2½ cups sugar

I teaspoon almond extract

4 eggs

2 tablespoons grated orange peel

I½ cups milk

4 cups unbleached white flour

4 teaspoons baking powder

I⅓ cups coarsely chopped almonds

I½ cups finely chopped dried apricots

GOAT CHEESE SPREAD

16 ounces fresh goat cheese

I cup heavy cream

½ teaspoon freshly ground black
    pepper

Preheat the oven to 350 degrees. Butter two 9 x 5-inch loaf pans.

Cream the butter and sugar in the bowl of an electric mixer until light. Add the almond extract, eggs, and orange peel. Mix well. Add the remaining ingredients, and mix at low speed until well blended.

Divide the batter between the buttered loaf pans. Bake for 1 hour, or until a toothpick inserted in the center of the loaves comes out clean. Cook for 15 minutes.

Remove the loaves from their pans, and cool completely. Wrap in foil and store in the refrigerator.

To make the spread, place all the ingredients in the bowl of an electric mixer fitted with the whisk attachment. Beat until smooth and fluffy.

To make the finger sandwiches, cut each loaf into 12 slices. Spread 6 of the slices with half the goat cheese mixture. Cover with the remaining 6 slices, and quarter each sandwich lengthwise. Repeat the procedure with the second loaf and the remaining half of the spread.

Arrange the finger sandwiches on a platter, and serve.

YIELD: 48 FINGER SANDWICHES.

Brussels Sprouts and Carrots with Niçoise Mayonnaise

Put the Brussels sprouts into a large pot that is half full of boiling water. Simmer, uncovered, for 3 minutes. Drain, and immediately plunge the sprouts into very cold water.

Store the Brussels sprouts and the raw carrots in a container in the refrigerator until ready to serve.

To make the mayonnaise, process the egg yolks in the bowl of a food processor fitted with a steel blade. With the processor running, add the lemon juice, salt, and pepper. Combine the 2 oils in a pitcher with a pouring spout. With the processor still running, add the oils in a very thin stream. The mayonnaise should be thick.

Turn off the processor, add the tuna, and process for 2 seconds. Add the olive purée, and pulse twice to blend. If the mayonnaise is too thick, add 1 or 2 tablespoons milk, and pulse to blend.

Transfer the mayonnaise to a small bowl, cover, and chill until ready to use.

To serve, arrange the vegetables in a pretty basket, and serve with the Niçoise Mayonnaise on the side.

YIELD: 30 SERVINGS.

5 pounds Brussels sprouts, trimmed
3 pounds carrots, peeled and cut into sticks

NIÇOISE MAYONNAISE

4 egg yolks, at room temperature
6 tablespoons lemon juice
1 teaspoon coarse salt
1 teaspoon freshly ground black pepper
1 cup safflower oil
1 cup olive oil
¾ cup canned white tuna
2 tablespoons black olive purée

Apple-Onion Tart

10 cups finely chopped red onions

1 cup extra-virgin olive oil

1½ tablespoons coarse salt

1½ teaspoons freshly ground black
pepper

2 teaspoons fresh thyme leaves, or
1 teaspoon dried

4 cups unbleached white flour

2 tablespoons active dry yeast

2 teaspoons sugar

1½ cups warm water

2½ pounds (5 or 6 whole) McIntosh
apples, peeled, cored, and sliced into
thin rings

½ pound Roquefort cheese

Over medium heat, sauté the onions in ¾ cup olive oil for about 15 minutes, or until they are soft. Stir in the salt, pepper, and thyme, and cool to room temperature.

Combine the flour, yeast, sugar, ¼ cup olive oil, and warm water in the bowl of an electric mixer. Beat at low speed until well mixed. Turn out onto a flour-dusted countertop. Knead the dough until smooth and elastic, about 8 to 10 minutes. Return to the bowl, cover, and let rise in a warm place for 30 minutes.

Preheat the oven to 375 degrees.

Roll the dough out to about ½ inch thick. Fit it into a 12 x 18-inch sheet pan, patting and stretching the dough to an even thickness. Cover the bottom with half of the sautéed onions. Add the apples, arranging them in slightly overlapping rows. Top with the remaining onions, distributing them evenly over the apple slices.

Bake for 30 to 35 minutes.

Just before serving, crumble the Roquefort cheese over the tart, and bake in a preheated 350-degree oven for 15 minutes. Cut into bite-size pieces.

YIELD: 30 SERVINGS, APPROXIMATELY 96 PIECES.

Gingersnaps

Cream the butter and sugar in the bowl of an electric mixer. Add the eggs and gingerroot. Beat until well combined. Add the flour, cloves, and baking soda. Mix at low speed until no pieces of flour remain. Chill the dough for 1 hour, or up to 24 hours.

Preheat the oven to 350 degrees. Lightly butter 2 baking sheets.

Roll the dough into ninety 1-inch balls, and place them on the prepared baking sheets, 2 inches apart. Top each cookie with 1 pecan half, and press down lightly.

Bake 12 to 14 minutes. Cool 5 minutes before removing from the pan. The cookies will remain crisp if stored in an airtight container.

10 ounces (2½ sticks) butter, softened
2 cups dark brown sugar
2 eggs
⅓ cup minced fresh gingerroot
3½ cups unbleached white flour
½ teaspoon ground cloves
2 teaspoons baking soda
6 ounces (approximately 90) pecan halves

YIELD: 90 COOKIES.

Chocolate Wedding Cake

In order for the flavors to fully blend, this cake should rest for at least 24 hours before the final frosting and decorating. If you wish, it can be made as many as 3 days before serving.

CAKE

1 pound semisweet chocolate
1 pound (4 sticks) butter, softened
4½ cups sugar
10 eggs
1 tablespoon vanilla extract
2⅔ cups milk
7 cups unbleached white flour
1 tablespoon baking soda

SUGAR SYRUP

1 cup water
½ cup sugar
½ cup Grand Marnier

CHOCOLATE FILLING

10 ounces semisweet chocolate
½ pound (2 sticks) butter, softened
2 tablespoons Grand Marnier

Preheat the oven to 325 degrees. Butter a 12-inch and a 9½-inch springform pan.

To make the cake, melt the chocolate in the top of a double boiler, over simmering water. Set aside to cool.

Cream the butter with the sugar in the bowl of an electric mixer until light. Add the eggs and vanilla. Beat to blend well.

Transfer the mixture to a larger mixing bowl and add the melted chocolate, milk, 2 cups of the flour, and the baking soda. Beat to mix well. Add the remaining flour, and blend.

Divide the batter between the 2 prepared springform pans, filling each a little more than half full. Smooth the tops.

Bake the 12-inch cake about 1 hour and 35 minutes. Bake the 9½-inch cake about 15 minutes less, or until a toothpick inserted in the center comes out clean. Cool.

To make the syrup, bring the water to a boil, add the sugar, and stir until dissolved. Cool, then add the Grand Marnier. Transfer to a bowl.

To make the chocolate filling, melt the chocolate in the top of a double boiler. Stir in the butter, 4 tablespoons at a time. Add the Grand Marnier, and stir to blend well.

To assemble the cakes, remove them from their pans and slice each cake horizontally into 3 layers. Set a 12-inch layer on a cake plate. Sprinkle with some of the Grand Marnier sugar syrup, then spread on a thin layer of chocolate filling. Top that with a second 12-inch layer, and repeat the process. After the third layer has been added, continue the process by adding the 9½-inch layers, centering them on top of the larger cake. Make sure you reserve enough Grand Marnier sugar syrup and chocolate filling to fill all six layers.

Store the cake, lightly covered in plastic, in the refrigerator until ready to frost.

On the day of the wedding, beat the heavy cream with the confectioners' sugar and vanilla until firm peaks hold. Spread most of the cream over the top and sides of the cake, covering the cake completely.

Spoon the remaining whipped cream into a pastry bag fitted with a star tip, and pipe the cream in a decorative pattern on the sides and outline of the cake. Decorate with fresh flowers.

Store the cake in a cool place until ready to serve. The cake can be completed up to 4 hours before serving.

YIELD: 30 TO 40 SERVINGS.

FROSTING

2 quarts heavy cream
1 cup confectioners' sugar
2 teaspoons vanilla extract
Fresh flowers for decoration

A COUNTRY LUNCH
FOR EIGHT

CORN CHOWDER

BREAD STICKS

WARM KALE SALAD

CRANBERRY-PEAR PIE

Surrounded by potato fields and cornfields, and only a short hop from the ocean and the Long Island Sound, we at Loaves and Fishes have come to regard chowders as one of our native specialties. Our fish chowders, clam chowders, and various bisques are made fresh at the start of every weekend, and are invariably sold out by Sunday evening. The most popular chowder of them all is our spicy Corn Chowder.

We thought that with the various holidays coming upon us in rapid succession, a menu for a quiet lunch, easy to prepare, might be just the sort of meal you would really appreciate.

The soup can be made the day before and refrigerated.

The bread sticks can be bought from a bakery or gourmet food store.

The Kale Salad and Cranberry-Pear Pie are simple to prepare the morning of the lunch.

Corn Chowder

Heat the bacon and olive oil in a large soup pot. Add the onions and pepper, and sauté for 10 minutes, or until the vegetables are transparent and the bacon is crisp. Stir in the flour, salt, and chili powder. Add the chicken stock and squash pieces, and stir well. Bring to a boil, lower the heat, and simmer, covered, for 30 minutes.

Add the cheese, corn, and cream. Bring to a boil and remove from the heat. Stir in ½ cup of coriander.

Serve in deep soup bowls, garnished with the remaining coriander.

YIELD: 8 TO 10 SERVINGS.

1 cup finely chopped bacon
2 tablespoons olive oil
3 cups finely chopped onions
1¼ cups (1 large) finely chopped green bell pepper
½ cup unbleached white flour
2 teaspoons coarse salt
1 teaspoon Mexican chili powder (more if you like it spicy)
10 cups chicken stock (page 8)
4 cups (1 medium) peeled, seeded, and cubed butternut squash
2 cups (½ pound) grated sharp cheddar cheese
4 cups fresh or frozen corn kernels
¾ cup heavy cream
¾ cup chopped fresh coriander

Warm Kale Salad

Heat the olive oil in a large sauté pan until hot but not smoking. Add the shallots, red wine vinegar, salt, pepper, and kale. Cook the kale a few minutes, tossing it several times, until it darkens slightly in color. Remove from the heat, and divide the kale among 8 salad plates.

Using the same pan, sauté the peppers and onions over medium heat for about 5 minutes, stirring three or four times. Spoon a little of the pepper-onion mixture over the top of each plate of kale. Serve immediately.

YIELD: 8 SERVINGS.

¾ cup olive oil
1 cup finely chopped shallots
3 tablespoons red wine vinegar
1½ teaspoons coarse salt
1 teaspoon freshly ground black pepper
2 pounds kale with large ribs discarded, torn into bite-size pieces
2 large red bell peppers, julienned
1 large red onion, cut into very thin rings

Cranberry-Pear Pie

PASTRY

2½ cups unbleached white flour
1 teaspoon sugar
½ teaspoon salt
½ pound (2 sticks) cold butter, cut into 16 pieces
2 tablespoons lemon juice
¼ cup cold water

FILLING

4 cups fresh or frozen cranberries
1½ pounds (4 medium) ripe pears, peeled, cored, and cut into thin wedges
1 tablespoon grated orange peel
½ teaspoon ground cinnamon
1½ cups sugar
¼ cup unbleached white flour

2 tablespoons butter, melted
3 tablespoons sugar

To make the pastry, place the flour, sugar, salt, and butter in the bowl of a food processor fitted with a steel blade. Pulse 6 times, or until the mixture resembles coarse meal. With the motor running, add the lemon juice and cold water. Process for about 10 seconds, or until the dough starts to form a ball.

Turn the dough out onto a flour-dusted countertop. Gather together the crumbs and form into a ball. Wrap the dough in plastic, and chill in the refrigerator for 30 minutes.

Place the filling ingredients in a large bowl. Toss to blend, and set aside.

Preheat the oven to 375 degrees. Butter a 10-inch pie plate.

Transfer the dough to the flour-dusted countertop, divide it in half, and roll out one half into a circle ⅛-inch thick and 12 inches in diameter. Fit the circle into the prepared pie plate. Trim the edges.

Spoon the filling into the pie shell.

Roll out the second piece of dough into an 11-inch circle, ⅛ inch thick. Cover the pie with this circle, and trim and crimp the edges. Cut 6 vent slits into the top crust. Brush with the melted butter and sprinkle with the sugar. Bake 50 minutes, or until the pie is evenly browned.

Serve warm or cool to room temperature.

NOTE: Covered and stored at room temperature, leftovers will keep for up to 2 days.

YIELD: 8 TO 10 SERVINGS.

CHRISTMAS EVE SUPPER
FOR EIGHT

When I was growing up, the rabbits my mother roasted for Christmas came from the fields around our farm. Once the rabbit had been skinned and cleaned, my mother would marinate it in wine and vinegar for at least 3 days. This would mellow the gamy taste and tenderize the meat. Then, on Christmas Eve morning, my mother would remove the rabbit from the marinade and braise it for hours in a mixture of herbs, wine, and garlic. The meat would soak up the garden of flavors and then be roasted to a brown crispness. My mother served the rabbit in a delectable mustard sauce, always impeccably moist and delicious.

The game we buy nowadays from our butcher shops is often tame and young. The meat is white, and has the texture of chicken. Marinating a store-bought rabbit for any more than 12 hours would certainly destroy the delicate meat.

Roast Rabbit with Lemon and Rosemary is a variation of my mother's recipe and the meat needs only to be marinated overnight. The actual roasting and dressing can take place 2 hours before serving time.

The Orange Tart should be made a day ahead. It's tangy and delicious, and a perfect dessert to serve with any game dish.

The scallops take no time to prepare, and should be broiled just minutes before they're to be eaten. The dressing can be made earlier in the day, and stored at room temperature.

Read over the recipes carefully before starting. Make sure you have everything you will need at your fingertips, because this is one of those festive occasions when it isn't easy to dash out to the grocery store to buy something you've forgotten to include on your shopping list. With a little extra care in planning, this could turn out to be one of the simplest yet most intriguing Christmas Eve dinners you've ever prepared.

WARM SCALLOPS ON A
BED OF ARUGULA

ROAST RABBIT WITH LEMON
AND ROSEMARY

MUSHROOM AND PEA SAUTÉ
WITH MINT

CRISP ROAST POTATOES

ORANGE TART

Warm Scallops on a Bed of Arugula

If you cannot buy arugula, substitute smooth spinach leaves. Served with a coarse-grained bread, this would make a wonderful lunch for 4.

1 cup unbleached white flour
½ cup bread crumbs
½ cup teaspoon cayenne
1½ teaspoons coarse salt
2 pounds bay scallops, or sea scallops cut in half
¼ pound (1 stick) butter
3 teaspoons minced garlic
10 cups (3 bunches) loosely packed arugula or any other bitter green

DRESSING

2 tablespoons red wine vinegar
½ cup extra-virgin olive oil
1 teaspoon coarse salt
1 teaspoon freshly ground black pepper

Preheat the broiler.

Combine the flour, bread crumbs, cayenne, and salt in a bowl. Add the scallops, and toss to coat. Transfer the scallops to a shallow roasting pan.

Melt the butter in a small saucepan and add the garlic. Sauté for 1 minute. Drizzle the mixture over the scallops, and broil for about 3 to 5 minutes, without turning, until just done.

Place the arugula leaves in a large bowl. Pour the dressing ingredients into a screw-top jar and shake to blend. Spoon over the arugula, and toss to coat.

Divide the greens among 8 appetizer plates. Top with warm scallops and serve.

YIELD: 8 FIRST-COURSE SERVINGS.

Roast Rabbit with Lemon and Rosemary

The rabbit pieces need to marinate overnight. Scented with fresh rosemary, sharpened with lemon, juniper berries, and onions, and dabbed with a creamy mustard sauce, the meat is succulent and tender.

Place the rabbit pieces in a glass or earthenware casserole. Pour the lemon juice over the rabbit, cover, and refrigerate overnight.

When ready to roast, preheat the oven to 325 degrees, and butter a roasting pan.

Remove the rabbit pieces from the casserole, discarding the juice. Sprinkle the rabbit with salt and pepper, and wrap a strip of bacon around each piece. Place all the rabbit pieces in the buttered roasting pan, except for the back pieces, which need less cooking time. Melt the butter, and pour half of it over the rabbit in the roasting pan.

Roast for 1 hour. Remove from the oven, and add the onions, celery, garlic, juniper berries, bay leaf, and rosemary, then return the roasting pan to the oven and roast 30 minutes more.

Heat the chicken stock and wine in a small saucepan, and pour over the rabbit in the roasting pan. Add the back pieces of rabbit, and pour the remaining butter over them. Roast 20 minutes more. Add the heavy cream, and roast 10 minutes more. Lower heat to 200 degrees.

Transfer the rabbit to a warm serving platter and place in the oven to keep warm while you make the sauce.

Strain the roasting pan juices, including all the brown bits scraped from the bottom of the pan, into a medium-size saucepan and place over medium heat.

Mix the potato starch with the mustard in a small bowl and pour into the sauce. Bring the sauce to a boil, stirring constantly.

To serve, ladle some sauce over the rabbit. Garnish the platter with rosemary sprigs and lemon wedges. Serve the remaining sauce on the side.

YIELD: 8 SERVINGS.

Two 4-pound rabbits, skinned and cut into serving pieces
1 cup lemon juice
1 tablespoon coarse salt
1½ teaspoons freshly ground black pepper
½ pound thinly sliced bacon
¼ pound (1 stick) butter
3 cups chopped onions
1½ cups chopped celery
3 teaspoons minced garlic
8 juniper berries, crushed
1 bay leaf
4 sprigs fresh rosemary

SAUCE

2½ cups chicken stock (page 8)
1½ cups dry white wine
1 cup heavy cream
1 tablespoon potato starch
2 tablespoons Dijon mustard

6 sprigs rosemary
2 lemons, cut into 8 pieces each

Mushroom and Pea Sauté with Mint

½ pound fresh porcini or chanterelle
  mushrooms, or ¼ pound dried
⅓ cup extra-virgin olive oil
1 pound fresh white mushrooms
3½ cups fresh or thawed frozen peas
¼ cup chopped fresh mint leaves
2 teaspoons coarse salt
1½ teaspoons freshly ground black
  pepper

If you are unable to find fresh porcini or chanterelle mushrooms, soften the dried mushrooms in 1 cup warm water for 15 minutes. Drain before proceeding.

Heat the olive oil in a large skillet. Add the mushrooms and sauté over high heat until lightly browned, about 5 minutes. Add the peas, and sauté 5 minutes more. Remove from the heat and add the mint, salt, and pepper. Stir to blend and serve at once.

YIELD: 8 SERVINGS.

Crisp Roast Potatoes

10 medium baking potatoes, peeled
¾ cup extra-virgin olive oil
1½ tablespoons coarse salt

Preheat the oven to 450 degrees.

Slice the potatoes very thinly and place in a mixing bowl. Pour the oil over them, and toss to coat well. Lay the potato slices, overlapping, in a large buttered baking sheet. Sprinkle with salt, and roast for about 20 minutes, or until crisp. Serve on the same plate with the rabbit.

NOTE: For a delicious variation, you can substitute duck fat for the olive oil in this recipe. Melt ½ cup of duck fat over low heat. Coat the potatoes, and roast to golden crispness.

YIELD: 8 SERVINGS.

Orange Tart

Allow the tart to chill overnight before serving. This will give the filling time to set and the flavors a chance to ripen.

Preheat the oven to 375 degrees.

To make the crust, place the flour, sugar, salt, and butter in the bowl of a food processor fitted with a steel blade. Pulse 6 times. Add the egg and the cream. Process until the dough forms a ball. Wrap in plastic, and chill for 30 minutes.

On a lightly floured countertop, roll the dough into a circle 11 inches in diameter, and about ⅛ inch thick. Fit the circle into a 9½-inch springform pan, pressing it 1 inch up the sides. Line the tart with foil, and fill with dried beans.

Bake 15 minutes. Remove the beans and foil.

To make the filling, place the eggs and 1½ cups of sugar in the large bowl of an electric mixer. Beat until foamy. Add the orange juice, orange peel, and lemon juice to the egg mixture. With the mixer running, pour in the melted butter. Blend well.

Pour the filling into the partly baked crust, and bake for 55 minutes, or until the custard is set. If the custard begins to brown, cover it with foil for the remaining baking time. Cool to room temperature.

Combine the remaining 1¼ cups of sugar with water, and bring to a boil. Add the orange slices, and simmer for 10 minutes. Remove from the heat and allow to cool slightly before covering the tart with the orange slices, arranging them in a slightly overlapping circular design. Discard the syrup. Cool to room temperature, cover the pie, and chill in the refrigerator overnight.

To serve, cut with a very sharp knife into 8 pieces.

YIELD: 8 SERVINGS.

CRUST

1½ cups unbleached white flour
¼ cup sugar
½ teaspoon salt
¼ pound (1 stick) cold butter, cut into 8 pieces
1 egg
2 tablespoons heavy cream

FILLING

4 eggs
1½ cups sugar
⅔ cup fresh orange juice
2 tablespoons grated orange peel
3 tablespoons lemon juice
6 tablespoons butter, melted
2 navel oranges, thinly sliced

1¼ cups sugar
1½ cups water

A DANISH CHRISTMAS BREAKFAST
FOR EIGHT

BAKED APPLES IN
VANILLA SYRUP

SOFT SCRAMBLED EGGS

SALMON CAKES

STOLLEN

This is the customary breakfast we enjoyed in Denmark every Christmas morning. Eggs fresh from our hens, savory fishcakes, baked apples, and the traditional Stollen, served with plenty of sweet butter . . . just the kind of breakfast to keep everyone nourished and satisfied until Christmas dinner.

The Stollen can be made up to 1 month before Christmas. Wrapped well and frozen, it can be defrosted the night before Christmas, and warmed in the oven just before you wish to serve it. It seems to be just enough time for the flavors to settle and blend. It's also a wonderful breakfast loaf year round.

The Salmon Cakes should be made 1 day ahead. Sauté them a few minutes before serving. If need be, pop them into the oven to keep warm while you're scrambling the eggs.

I suggest that you bake the apples that morning, so they're still warm when you bring them to the table.

Gläde Jul!

Baked Apples in Vanilla Syrup

A traditional way to prepare our palates for a savory breakfast on a cold winter morning was to start with something warm and sweet. These buttery baked apples will also double as a delicious dinner dessert any time of the year.

Preheat the oven to 375 degrees.

Pour the water into a medium saucepan, add the lemon juice, sugar, and vanilla bean, and bring to a boil. Reduce the heat, cover, and simmer for 5 minutes. Set aside.

Stem and core the apples. Peel only the top half of each apple, leaving the peel on the bottom half. Arrange the apples in an oven-to-table casserole. Place 1½ teaspoons butter in the cavity of each apple, and pour the vanilla syrup around the apples. Bake 45 minutes, or until tender.

Serve warm.

3 cups water
3 tablespoons lemon juice
1½ cups sugar
1 vanilla bean, split in half lengthwise
8 baking apples (Rome Beauty or Cortland)
4 tablespoons butter

YIELD: 8 SERVINGS.

Soft Scrambled Eggs

Break the eggs into a large mixing bowl. Beat well. Add the milk, pepper, and salt. Stir to blend.

Heat the butter in a large skillet. Pour the egg mixture into the pan, and cook over medium heat, stirring gently for 2 to 3 minutes, or until the eggs are just set.

20 large eggs
¾ cup milk
¾ teaspoon freshly ground black pepper
1½ teaspoons coarse salt
6 tablespoons butter

YIELD: 8 SERVINGS.

Salmon Cakes

Crisp on the outside; moist, tender, and savory inside; served with a rich, leafy green salad; sprinkled with a tangy vinaigrette, these Salmon Cakes could double as an ideal light lunch.

3 pounds boneless fresh salmon

½ cup finely chopped onion

2 egg whites

2 teaspoons Dijon mustard

¾ teaspoon freshly ground black pepper

⅛ teaspoon Tabasco

2 teaspoons coarse salt

1 cup heavy cream

1 cup finely chopped chives or scallion tops

½ cups unbleached white flour

2 cups peanut oil

Cut one-third of the salmon into ¼-inch cubes and set aside. Place the remaining salmon in the bowl of a food processor fitted with a steel blade. Add the onion, egg whites, mustard, black pepper, Tabasco, and salt. Process until finely chopped, about 5 seconds. Transfer the mixture to a large mixing bowl and add the cubed salmon pieces.

Whip the heavy cream until soft peaks hold. Add half the chives, and fold the whipped cream into the salmon mixture.

Dust a baking sheet with half of the flour.

Using 2 tablespoons per cake, carefully shape the soft salmon mixture into 16 patties, about 2 inches round and 1¼ inches thick. Place them on the prepared baking sheet, and sprinkle each patty with the remaining flour. Cover with plastic wrap, and chill for at least 2 hours, or overnight.

Heat the oil in a large sauté pan over medium heat until hot, but not smoking. Sauté the salmon cakes in batches, about 3 minutes on each side.

Place the cakes on the same serving platter with the scrambled eggs. Sprinkle with the remaining chives, and serve warm.

YIELD: 8 SERVINGS.

Stollen

Gently sweetened with sugar, raisins, and dried cherries, enriched with almonds, spiced with cardamom, with tangy overtones of lemon and orange, this Christmas loaf is at its best when made at least 2 days prior to serving. And it is simply wonderful toasted!

Dissolve the yeast and 1 teaspoon of the sugar in the warm water and set aside.

Melt 8 tablespoons of the butter in a heavy saucepan over low heat. Off heat, add the remaining ⅓ cup of sugar, the salt, and milk. Stir constantly over low heat, until the sugar and salt have dissolved, and the liquid is lukewarm.

Pour the mixture into the bowl of an electric mixer. Add the eggs, 2 cups of the flour, and the cardamom. Beat at medium speed for 2 minutes. Add the yeast, and beat 2 minutes more. Add another 2 cups of flour, the lemon peel, orange peel, raisins, cherries, and almonds. Beat at low speed for 3 minutes. Turn the dough out onto a floured countertop. Using the remaining ⅓ cup of flour, knead until smooth and elastic, about 3 minutes.

Grease a mixing bowl with 2 tablespoons of butter. Put the dough in the buttered bowl, and turn it once to coat it with butter. Cover with a cloth, and let rise in a warm place until doubled, about 2 hours.

Grease a baking sheet.

Turn the dough out onto a floured countertop, and divide it in half. Using your palms, press each half into a 10 x 6-inch rectangle. Fold the long side over to within 1 inch of the opposite edge to make a long, thin loaf. Seal by pressing lightly along the edge. Transfer both loaves to the prepared baking sheet. Let rise in a warm place until doubled in bulk, about 1 hour.

Preheat the oven to 375 degrees.

Bake the stollen for 35 to 40 minutes. When done, it should be nicely browned and sound hollow when tapped.

Melt the remaining 4 tablespoons of butter. Brush the hot loaves with the melted butter, dust with the confectioners' sugar, and allow to cool completely. Wrap the cooled stollen tightly in plastic and refrigerate.

1 tablespoon active dry yeast
⅓ cup plus 1 teaspoon sugar
¼ cup warm water
14 tablespoons (1¾ sticks) butter
1½ teaspoons salt
1 cup milk
2 eggs at room temperature
4⅓ cups unbleached white flour
1 tablespoon ground cardamom
¾ tablespoon minced lemon peel
1 tablespoon minced orange peel
1 cup raisins
¾ cup dry cherries (or currants)
1 cup slivered almonds
1 cup confectioners' sugar

YIELD: 2 STOLLEN, 20 SLICES.

CHRISTMAS DINNER

FOR EIGHT

APPLE AND BUTTERNUT SQUASH SOUP

ROAST GOOSE IN PARTS

LINGENBERRY KOMPOTT

PORCINI MUSHROOM AND BROCCOLI SAUTÉ

NUSS KNÖDEL (NUT DUMPLINGS)

PRUNE SOUFFLÉ

GRAND MARNIER CRÈME

FLAKY SUGAR COOKIES

This is a wonderful way to prepare your Christmas goose, because serving it in parts will help eliminate a lot of work before, during, and after dinner. Ask your butcher to cut close to the bone and remove the breast meat for you. You'll need the legs and thighs separated. Also, ask him to cut away as much of the fat as he can, so you can use it for sautéeing, frying, or roasting almost any potato dish or vegetable. Save the carcass for your stock.

The Lingenberry Kompott and Nuss Knödel are recipes from my mother's well-worn file. The instructions on her kompott merely called for "amounts of sugar and vinegar to taste. The harvests were different from year to year," she explained. "Sometimes the berries were sweet, and other years they were not so good. I would use them anyway, and compensate by using more sugar." You can make the Lingenberry Kompott 2 days ahead and refrigerate it. Chilled slightly, it serves as a wonderful relish for any pork or poultry dish.

The soup, Grand Marnier Crème, and cookies can all be made 1 day in advance. The soup and Crème will need refrigeration, but the cookies are fine wrapped and left at room temperature.

The goose parts have to be placed in their marinade the night before. This would also be a good time to make the stock from the bones the butcher gave you.

On the day you plan to serve this meal, prepare the prune purée and ramekins for the soufflé early in the day. Beat and fold in the egg whites just before baking.

Covered in foil, the Nuss Knödel (poached dumplings) can be kept warm in a 200-degree oven for up to an hour before serving the meal.

This meal can easily be doubled to serve 16.

Apple and Butternut Squash Soup

Place the first 3 ingredients in a large soup pot. Add the chicken stock, salt, pepper, rosemary, and thyme. Bring to a boil, reduce the heat, and simmer for 45 minutes.

Remove from the heat, stir in the heavy cream, and allow the soup to cool slightly. Using a blender, purée the soup mixture in batches.

To serve, bring the soup back to a boil and heat through. Cut the apple into thin slices, dipping each slice in the lemon juice to keep it from discoloring. Float 1 slice in each bowl of soup. Sprinkle with thyme.

YIELD: 8 TO 10 SERVINGS.

3½ pounds (3 medium) butternut squash, peeled, seeded, and cut into 2-inch cubes
2 pounds (4 medium) tart apples, peeled, cored, and cut into 2-inch cubes
2½ cups coarsely chopped onions
8 cups chicken stock (page 8)
2 teaspoons coarse salt
1 teaspoon freshly ground black pepper
1 teaspoon dried rosemary
¾ teaspoon dried thyme
½ cup heavy cream

GARNISH

1 tart apple
¼ cup lemon juice
2 tablespoons minced fresh thyme

Roast Goose in Parts

The goose parts should marinate for at least 2 hours, but for no longer than 6 before you begin your cooking. Each piece is golden brown and crispy on the outside, and moist and tender inside.

Two 12 to 13-pound fresh geese
½ cup olive oil
2 cups port wine
1 teaspoon dried thyme
3 large onions, cut in half
Water
2 carrots, cut in half
1 stalk celery, cut in 4 pieces
10 sprigs parsley
2 bay leaves
2 teaspoons coarse salt
Freshly ground black pepper
4 teaspoons arrowroot
Holiday greens for garnish

For those of you who would prefer carving the poultry yourself, instead of having your butcher do it, here is how to proceed:

Remove all visible fat from the inside of the birds, and save for sautéeing or frying. Cutting close to the bone, remove the breast meat. Remove the legs, and separate the leg and thigh.

Pour the olive oil and 1½ cups of port wine into a large earthenware casserole. Add the thyme. Place the goose parts in the marinade, turning to coat them well. Cover the casserole and refrigerate until ready to roast.

Using a cleaver, cut the carcasses into several pieces. Place them in a large stockpot. Add the onions, and, over medium heat, brown the bones about 30 minutes.

Add enough cold water to the stockpot to cover the bones by 2 inches. Add the carrots, celery, parsley, bay leaves, salt, and pepper. Bring to a rolling boil, reduce the heat, and simmer, partially covered, for 3 hours. Discard the bones, and reduce the stock over medium heat until about 6 cups remain; this will take about 45 minutes.

Preheat the oven to 450 degrees.

Distribute the goose parts in 2 roasting pans. Sprinkle with salt and pepper, and roast for 30 minutes. Reduce the oven temperature to 350 degrees. Cover the meat with foil, and roast an additional 45 minutes.

To make the sauce, strain 6 cups of stock into a saucepan. Dissolve the arrowroot with the remaining ½ cup of port wine, and add to the stock. Bring the stock to a boil, stirring constantly. Add salt and pepper to taste. When it begins to thicken, remove from the heat.

To serve, carve the breast pieces on the diagonal. Arrange all the meat on a warm serving platter. Garnish with holly, or other holiday greens. Pass the sauce separately.

YIELD: 8 TO 10 SERVINGS.

Lingenberry Kompott

This tart-sweet relish is a ravishing complement to any poultry dish and is also great with pork.

Empty the lingenberries with their juice into a small saucepan. Add the remaining ingredients, and stir over low heat until the mixture starts to bubble. Cool to room temperature. Chill until ready to use.

YIELD: 3½ CUPS.

Two 10-ounce jars lingenberries with
   sugar
6 cardamom pods, crushed
1 cup packed brown sugar
3 tablespoons apple cider vinegar
½ teaspoon salt
½ teaspoon freshly ground black
   pepper

Porcini Mushroom and Broccoli Sauté

Porcini mushrooms have a deep and distinctive flavor that blends perfectly with vegetables that have a robust taste.

Heat the olive oil in a large sauté pan. Add the onions and sauté for about 5 minutes, until they become transparent. Add the mushrooms and broccoli. Sauté for 5 minutes, stirring often. Season with salt and pepper before serving.

YIELD: 8 TO 10 SERVINGS.

3 tablespoons olive oil
2 medium onions, thinly sliced
½ pound fresh porcini or white
   mushrooms, thinly sliced
10 cups (2 heads) broccoli florets
Coarse salt and freshly ground black
   pepper

Nuss Knödel (Nut Dumplings)

We always served these delicious dumplings with stews, casseroles, and soups. They can easily replace potatoes in almost any meal.

7 cups cubed stale white bread
1¾ cups boiling hot milk
¾ cup finely chopped lean bacon
1½ cups finely chopped onions
½ cup finely ground pecans
½ cup finely ground hazelnuts
½ teaspoon cayenne
1 tablespoon coarse salt
¼ teaspoon ground nutmeg
½ teaspoon ground coriander
4 eggs
¼ cup finely chopped fresh parsley

Place the cubed bread in a large mixing bowl. Pour the hot milk over the bread and let it soak for 30 minutes.

In a small skillet, sauté the bacon until crisp. Add the onions, and sauté for 5 minutes. Pour over the bread. Add the remaining ingredients, except the parsley, and using your hands, mix thoroughly.

Fill a large skillet two-thirds full of water and bring to a boil.

Divide the dumpling mixture into 24 equal portions. Using your hands, roll each portion into a ball 1½ inches in diameter. Drop the balls into the simmering water, and cook for about 5 minutes.

Remove the dumplings with a slotted spoon and place on a plate lined with a white cloth napkin. Sprinkle with parsley and serve warm.

YIELD: 24 DUMPLINGS.

Prune Soufflé

Place the prunes, red wine, and sugar in a heavy saucepan, bring to a boil, reduce the heat, and simmer, covered, for 15 minutes. Cool for 30 minutes.

Spoon the prune mixture with its liquid into the bowl of a food processor fitted with a steel blade. Add the lemon juice, and process until smooth. Scrape the prune purée into a large mixing bowl.

Preheat the oven to 400 degrees. Butter and sugar eight 1-cup ramekins or an 8-cup soufflé dish.

Beat the egg whites in an electric mixer until soft peaks hold. Fold into the prune mixture.

Divide the soufflé among the prepared ramekins or fill the soufflé dish, heaping the center slightly. To help the center rise, run your finger in a circle about ½ inch from the edge of the dish.

Transfer the ramekins to a baking sheet. Bake 15 minutes. Dust the confectioners' sugar, and serve with the Grand Marnier Crème on the side.

1 pound pitted prunes
1½ cups red wine
½ cup sugar
3 tablespoons lemon juice
10 egg whites
¼ cup confectioners' sugar
Melted butter and some sugar to prepare ramekins

YIELD: 8 SERVINGS.

Grand Marnier Crème

This Grand Marnier Crème is a light and luscious accompaniment to the Prune Soufflé and also goes superbly with poached pears and figs or baked apples.

6 egg yolks
½ cup sugar
2 teaspoons cornstarch
4 cups milk
2 tablespoons butter
1 tablespoon grated orange peel
⅓ cup fresh orange juice
2 tablespoons Grand Marnier

Place the egg yolks, sugar, and cornstarch in a medium-size heavy saucepan. Beat with a wire whisk until light. Add milk and stir to blend.

Over medium heat, stirring constantly, bring the mixture almost to a boil. Remove from the heat, add the butter, and keep stirring to cool the custard.

Add the orange peel, juice, and Grand Marnier.

Chill in a pitcher until ready to serve.

YIELD: 5 CUPS.

Flaky Sugar Cookies

For variations of these melt-in-your-mouth cookies, try adding 1 teaspoon vanilla extract or ⅛ teaspoon almond extract to the batter; for a delicious tart cookie, mix in 2 teaspoons grated lemon peel or 1 tablespoon grated orange peel.

Process the flour and frozen butter in the bowl of a food processor fitted with a steel blade for 10 seconds. Add the crème fraîche, and process 5 seconds more.

Turn the dough out onto a countertop and gather into a ball. Cover with plastic and chill for 30 minutes.

Preheat the oven to 375 degrees. Butter a baking sheet.

On a lightly floured countertop, roll out the dough ⅛-inch thick. Using a 1½-inch round cookie cutter, cut out as many cookies as possible. Gather into a ball and roll out the scraps and cut more cookies.

Place the cookies on the prepared baking sheet, ¾ inch apart.

With a fork, beat together the egg yolk and cream until smooth. Brush each cookie top with the mixture, then sprinkle each one with sugar. Bake 8 to 10 minutes, or until the edges are light brown. Cool, and store the cookies in an airtight container.

2 cups unbleached white flour
12 tablespoons (1½ sticks) frozen
    butter, cut into 24 pieces
¾ cup crème fraîche (page 9)
1 egg yolk
1 tablespoon heavy cream or milk
¾ cup sugar

YIELD: 32 COOKIES.

NEW YEAR'S EVE DINNER
FOR TWELVE

MUSHROOM TART

SMOKED TROUT
WITH FENNEL

OVEN-BRAISED PHEASANT
WITH PEARS

TWICE-COOKED GREEN BEANS

POTATO AND PARSNIP
GRATIN

POACHED MERINGUES WITH
ALMOND CUSTARD

COCOA BARS

In Holland, Denmark, and Northern Germany, New Year's Eve is called *Sylvester,* after Saint Sylvester. Children, bundled up against the cold, go from door to door singing a traditional song in which they ask for "little cakes."

I remember the excitement of those evenings: my fingers numb from the cold, the snow crunching under my boots as I raced for home, opening the door to a rush of welcoming aromas from the feast my mother was preparing, showing her how many cakes I had to share. Then I would sit with my family around a long table next to the fireplace, remembering the joy and appreciation we felt as the food was brought out. We'd hold hands for a moment, giving thanks for the past year—grateful to be welcoming in the New Year, together.

Here is one of those meals, adapted to make it as simple as possible.

The mushroom tart filling, except for the eggs and milk, can be prepared the day before New Year's Eve.

The tart crust and Cocoa Bars can be made the day before. The Potato and Parsnip Gratin can be assembled up to 1 day ahead and then baked 1 hour before serving time.

The meringues can be poached up to 6 hours before dinner and stored, covered, in the refrigerator. Everything else should be made the day of the party.

This is a completely satisfying, delicious meal that I have transported from my mother's kitchen to my own.

Mushroom Tart

Place the flour, cold butter, salt, and pepper in the bowl of a food processor fitted with a steel blade. Pulse 5 times. Add the lemon juice, and process until the dough forms a ball. Wrap in plastic, and chill for 30 minutes.

Preheat the oven to 375 degrees. Butter a 17 x 12 x 1-inch baking sheet.

Roll the dough into a 18 x 13-inch rectangle, ⅛ inch thick. Fit the dough into the prepared baking sheet, pushing up around the sides until it reaches the top edge of the sheet. Line the pastry with foil and fill with dried beans. Bake 15 minutes. Remove the beans and foil, and bake 5 minutes more.

In the processor bowl, process the shallots and mushrooms in several batches until finely chopped.

Melt the butter in a large sauté pan. Add the mushroom-shallot mixture, and sauté over medium heat, stirring until all the liquid had evaporated. Cut the cream cheese into small pieces and add it to the mushrooms, along with the cayenne and salt. Continue stirring until the cream cheese melts. Remove from the heat, and cool to room temperature.

Preheat the oven to 350 degrees.

Beat the eggs and milk until well combined. Pour into the mushroom mixture and stir to blend. Pour the filling into the prebaked crust, spreading evenly and smoothing the top.

Bake 30 to 35 minutes, or until set.

Let the tart cool for 15 minutes before cutting it into 2-inch squares. Sprinkle with parsley and serve.

CRUST

2½ cups unbleached white flour
½ pound (2 sticks) cold butter, cut into 16 pieces
½ teaspoon salt
½ teaspoon freshly ground black pepper
3 tablespoons lemon juice

FILLING

1½ cups coarsely chopped shallots
3 pounds mushrooms
6 tablespoons butter
8 ounces cream cheese
½ teaspoon cayenne
2 teaspoons coarse salt
3 eggs
1 cup milk

½ cup finely chopped fresh parsley

YIELD: APPROXIMATELY 50 SQUARES.

Smoked Trout with Fennel

4 fennel bulbs
2 cups chicken stock (page 8)

DRESSING

1 cup extra-virgin olive oil
5 tablespoons red wine vinegar
2 tablespoons Dijon mustard
1¼ teaspoons coarse salt
¾ teaspoon freshly ground black
    pepper
6 small smoked trout, about 12 ounces
    each, skinned and boned

Cut away the stalks and feathery fronds of the fennel, and save them for garnish. Cut each bulb into ¼-inch strips.

In a medium-size saucepan, heat the chicken stock. Add the fennel, and bring to a boil. Reduce the heat, and simmer 4 to 5 minutes. Drain. Save and freeze the cooking liquid for your stockpot.

Combine the dressing ingredients in a screw-top jar. Shake vigorously to blend.

To serve, divide the fennel among 12 first-course plates. Add half a trout to each plate. Drizzle the dressing over each salad, and garnish with snippets of fennel fronds.

YIELD: 12 SERVINGS AS A FIRST COURSE.

Oven-Braised Pheasant with Pears

Preheat the oven to 450 degrees.

Rub each pheasant inside and out with ½ teaspoon of salt and ¼ teaspoon freshly ground black pepper.

Brown the bacon in a large sauté pan. Remove from the pan, and set aside. Discard all but ¼ cup of bacon fat.

Add the olive oil to the bacon fat and heat. Brown the pheasants on all sides by fitting them in the sauté pan 2 at a time. Transfer the pheasants to a large roasting pan and set aside.

Stir the onions into the same pan, and sauté until light brown. Add the garlic, thyme, porcini, white wine, and chicken stock. Bring the mixture to a boil, scraping up all the brown bits from the bottom of the pan. Pour into the roasting pan around the pheasants, and cover with foil. Braise the pheasants in the oven for 50 minutes.

Combine the port wine, peppercorns, and sugar in a medium-size saucepan, and bring to a boil. Add the pears, and reduce the heat. Cover and simmer until tender, about 20 minutes. Transfer the pears to a shallow roasting pan, leaving the port wine mixture in the saucepan. Over medium heat, reduce the port wine mixture until 1 cup remains. It should have a slightly syrupy consistency. Pour half over the pears, saving the other half for the sauce.

Transfer the pheasants to 2 large serving platters, reserving their juices for the sauce. Cover and keep warm in a 200-degree oven.

Place the pears, uncovered, in the warm oven while making the sauce.

Strain the pheasant juices into a saucepan, and discard the solids. Add the remaining port wine syrup and the heavy cream. Dissolve the arrowroot in the water, and add that to the sauce, stirring constantly. Bring the sauce to a boil over medium heat, remove from the heat, and adjust the seasoning to taste.

To serve, halve the pheasants with poultry shears. Garnish the platter with the pears, branches of thyme, and crisp bacon strips. Pass the sauce separately.

6 small pheasants, about 1½ to 1¾ pounds each

1 tablespoon coarse salt

1½ teaspoons freshly ground black pepper

8 ounces lean sliced bacon

¼ cup olive oil

3 cups chopped onions

4 teaspoons minced garlic

1½ teaspoons dried thyme

2 ounces dried porcini mushrooms

1½ cups dry white wine

2½ cups chicken stock (page 8)

2 cups port wine

6 black peppercorns, crushed

½ cup sugar

6 Bosc pears, peeled, halved, and cored

¾ cup heavy cream

2 teaspoons arrowroot

1½ tablespoons water

Fresh thyme branches

YIELD: 12 SERVINGS.

Twice-Cooked Green Beans

3 pounds fresh green beans, ends removed
¾ cup olive oil
3 teaspoons minced garlic
1 teaspoon red pepper flakes
2 teaspoons coarse salt

In a large pot of boiling water, blanch the beans for about 4 minutes, or until they are bright green. Drain, and quickly plunge them into ice-cold water to stop the cooking process.

Heat the olive oil in a large sauté pan. Add the beans, garlic, red pepper flakes, and salt. Sauté over medium-high heat for about 7 to 8 minutes, or until the beans are heated through and still crisp.

YIELD: 12 SERVINGS.

Potato and Parsnip Gratin

4 pounds baking potatoes, peeled and thinly sliced
4 pounds parsnips, peeled and thinly sliced
4 teaspoons minced garlic
8 tablespoons (1 stick) butter, melted
1½ tablespoons salt
2 teaspoons freshly ground black pepper
2½ cups heavy cream
2½ cups milk

Preheat the oven to 375 degrees.

Layer the sliced potatoes and parsnips alternately in a shallow 3½-quart casserole, trickling each layer with a combination of the garlic, melted butter, salt, and pepper. Top the casserole with a final layer of potatoes.

In a small saucepan, heat the cream and milk until very hot and pour over the casserole.

Bake 50 minutes, or until the potatoes and parsnips are tender.

YIELD: 12 SERVINGS.

Poached Meringues with Almond Custard

Light and airy meringues, floating on a silky custard sauce, delicately flavored with almonds.

Place the egg whites, cream of tartar, and ½ teaspoon of the almond extract into the bowl of an electric mixer. Beat at medium speed until foamy. With the machine running at high speed, add 1¼ cups of the sugar by pouring in a slow stream. Beat until firm peaks hold.

Pour 6 cups of milk into a large sauté pan, 12 inches in diameter and about 3 inches high. Dissolve 2 tablespoons of sugar in the milk, and bring to a simmer. Spoon heaping tablespoons of meringue in batches of 5 on top of the milk. Poach the meringues at a simmer, for 3 minutes on each side, turning them once and making sure the milk doesn't boil.

Remove the poached meringues with a slotted spoon, and place on a baking sheet lined with a kitchen towel. Cover with plastic wrap, and refrigerate until ready to serve.

To make the almond custard, combine the egg yolks with 1 cup of sugar in a heavy saucepan and beat with a wire whisk until creamy. Add the heavy cream and 5 cups of the poaching milk. Place over a medium-high heat, and stir constantly until the mixture is steaming hot but not boiling. It should be just beginning to thicken. Remove from the heat and continue stirring for about 5 minutes, to cool the custard. Stir in ¾ teaspoon of almond extract. Pour into a serving pitcher, and chill for 6 hours.

In a large skillet, toast the almonds with the remaining 2 tablespoons of sugar over medium heat. Toss frequently, until light brown.

To serve, spoon the Almond Custard onto 12 serving plates, or rimmed soup plates. Gently ladle 2 meringues onto each plate, sprinkle with toasted almonds, and serve.

10 eggs at room temperature, separated
½ teaspoon cream of tartar
1¼ teaspoons almond extract
2½ cups sugar
6 cups milk
1 cup heavy cream
1½ cups sliced almonds, skin intact

YIELD: 12 SERVINGS.

Cocoa Bars

1½ cups unbleached white flour
½ cup unsweetened cocoa
⅔ cup sugar
½ teaspoon baking powder
12 tablespoons (1½ sticks) cold butter,
    cut into small pieces
1 egg
1 teaspoon vanilla extract

Preheat the oven to 350 degrees.

Place the flour, cocoa, sugar, baking powder, and butter in the bowl of a food processor fitted with a steel blade. Process for 10 seconds, or until the dry ingredients and butter are well combined. Add the egg and vanilla, and pulse 3 times. Transfer the dough to a countertop, and using your hands, work into a ball.

Divide the dough into 3 equal pieces, and shape each piece into a long roll, about ¾ inch thick. Place the rolls on an ungreased baking sheet, 2 inches apart. Press down lightly to slightly flatten each roll.

Bake 15 to 20 minutes, or until the rolls spring back when lightly touched.

While the rolls are still warm, cut them diagonally into 1-inch-wide bars. Cool the bars to room temperature.

Stored in an airtight container, the bars will keep for up to 3 days.

YIELD: 24 BARS.

NEW YEAR'S DAY OPEN HOUSE
FOR THIRTY

We find New Year's Day to be the ideal occasion to bring together old and new friends, in an atmosphere that's both relaxed and inviting.

Cover a large buffet table with crisp linen and decorate it with dramatic sprays of pine and holly—the feast can act as your centerpiece. If you like, create a winter wreath of dried flowers, pine cones, cinnamon sticks, and cloves. It gives the room a deliciously spicy scent.

Pepper-Crusted Fillets of Beef may sound extravagant, but trimmed and prepared this way, every ounce is consumed and appreciated. We make approximately 40 fillets a weekend at Loaves and Fishes, and this is our foolproof recipe for baking them to a perfect, juicy rosiness every time. It's the least fatty meat you can buy, and I find that friends as well as customers prefer it for just this reason.

Shrimp in Sesame Dressing is always a crowd pleaser. This recipe is very exciting because of its adaptability. It is delicious served as part of a buffet or as hors d'oeuvres using the Sesame Dressing as a dipping sauce. The shrimp are also excellent as a first course when served on a bed of fresh, peppery arugula.

Much of this meal can be made well in advance of the gathering. For instance, the bread, Pear and Cranberry Relish, and the dressing for the salad can all be made up to 3 days before the party. The Orange-Currant Cake and the Sacher Torte are actually best when made 3 days in advance, as this gives their unique flavors time to blend.

The day before, you can prepare the Black-eyed Pea and Artichoke Salad, up to the point of adding the arugula. Store everything in the refrigerator until it's time to make the final additions.

PEPPER-CRUSTED
FILLETS OF BEEF WITH
HORSERADISH SAUCE

BLACK-EYED PEA AND
ARTICHOKE SALAD

SHRIMP IN
SESAME DRESSING

SALAD OF WINTER GREENS,
ENDIVE, APPLE,
AND RED PEPPER

PEAR AND CRANBERRY
RELISH

CRUSTY OAT BERRY BREAD

LINZER SCHNITTEN

ORANGE-CURRANT CAKE

SACHER TORTE

The Linzer Schnitten should be done the morning of your party.

The fillets, since they take so little time to roast, can be popped into the oven 1 hour before your guests arrive, leaving time for the meat to rest, and for you to slice and garnish the fillets.

It's a casual party with an elegant and festive menu . . . a wonderful way of welcoming in the New Year.

Pepper-Crusted Fillets of Beef with Horseradish Sauce

The creamy Horseradish Sauce needs to be refrigerated for at least 1 hour prior to serving, to allow the flavors to fully blend.

3 fillets of beef, about 3½ pounds each after trimming
¼ cup olive oil
2 teaspoons coarse salt
½ cup crushed black peppercorns

HORSERADISH SAUCE

2 cups heavy cream, whipped until soft peaks hold
3 cups sour cream
¾ cup minced fresh horseradish, or ⅓ cup drained bottled horseradish
¾ teaspoon salt
¼ teaspoon cayenne

¼ cup chopped fresh parsley

Preheat the oven to 500 degrees.

Rub the meat with the olive oil and sprinkle with salt and pepper. Place the fillets in a foil-lined roasting pan.

Bake for 20 minutes, uncovered. Remove from the oven and immediately cover with foil. Let the meat rest for 20 minutes.

To make the sauce, place all the ingredients in a small bowl, and fold to blend. Store in the refrigerator for at least 1 hour, or overnight. Just before serving, slice the meat thinly and arrange on a serving platter. Sprinkle with parsley.

Serve with the Horseradish Sauce on the side.

NOTE: Covered and refrigerated, the Horseradish Sauce will keep for up to 2 days.

YIELD: 40 SLICES, 6 CUPS SAUCE.

Black-eyed Pea and Artichoke Salad

Black-eyed peas for good luck!

To prepare the black-eyed peas, place all the ingredients in a 6-quart pot with 8 cups of cold water. Bring to a boil, and simmer for 20 to 30 minutes, until the peas are al dente. Drain, and set aside to cool slightly.

Combine the dressing ingredients in a screw-top jar, and shake vigorously. Pour two-thirds over the peas and toss to blend.

To make the salad, heat the olive oil, and sauté the garlic and artichoke hearts for 5 minutes. Remove from the heat, and allow to cool slightly.

Place the black-eyed peas in a large mixing bowl. Discard the cooked bacon, bay leaf, and celery. Add the sliced red onion rings and finely chopped raw celery.

Just before serving, add the fresh arugula. Sprinkle with the remaining vinaigrette, and toss lightly.

YIELD: 30 SERVINGS.

BLACK-EYED PEAS

1½ pounds dried black-eyed peas
8 ounces bacon, cut into 2-inch pieces
1 large onion, peeled and quartered
3 cloves garlic, mashed
1 bay leaf
1 stalk celery
1½ teaspoons coarse salt

DRESSING

6 tablespoons red wine vinegar
1 cup olive oil
1 tablespoon Dijon mustard
1 tablespoon coarse salt
2 teaspoons freshly ground black
  pepper

SALAD

¼ cup olive oil
2 teaspoons minced garlic
4 cups drained and quartered canned
  artichoke hearts
1 large red onion, cut into thin rings
2 cups finely chopped celery
2½ cups (2 bunches) fresh arugula,
  washed and dried

Shrimp in Sesame Dressing

¼ cup peanut oil

8 pounds fresh shrimp, shelled

2 tablespoons minced garlic

½ cup peeled and minced gingerroot

2 bunches scallions, finely chopped

DRESSING

2 cloves garlic, minced

2 teaspoons Dijon mustard

2 egg yolks

¼ cup sherry vinegar

¾ cup soy sauce

1 cup sesame oil

3 cups safflower oil

1 large head Romaine lettuce, shredded

Heat the peanut oil in a large skillet. Sauté the shrimp in batches, being sure not to crowd the pan. Stir each batch over medium heat for about 5 minutes. Add the garlic, gingerroot, and scallions, and sauté 1 minute more. Transfer to a large mixing bowl.

To make the dressing, place the garlic, mustard, egg yolks, sherry vinegar, and soy sauce in the bowl of a food processor fitted with a steel blade. Process for 2 seconds. With the processor running, add the sesame and safflower oils in a steady stream.

Pour the dressing over the shrimp. Mix gently. Transfer to a large serving platter lined with shredded lettuce.

YIELD: 30 SERVINGS.

Salad of Winter Greens, Endive, Apple, and Red Pepper

Wash and spin-dry the lettuce. Roll up the leaves and cut into ½-inch strips. Also cut the endive in the same fashion.

Place the greens, endive, red pepper, and apple pieces in a large salad bowl.

To make the dressing, combine all the ingredients in a screw-top jar. Shake well to blend, and pour over the greens. Toss lightly, and serve.

YIELD: 30 SERVINGS.

SALAD

2 heads winter greens, either chicory, romaine, or escarole
4 heads endive
4 red bell peppers, coarsely chopped
3 Golden Delicious apples, peel intact, cored and cut into ½-inch pieces

DRESSING

½ cup olive oil
¼ cup walnut oil
¼ cup white wine vinegar
⅛ teaspoon Tabasco
½ teaspoon freshly ground black pepper
I teaspoon coarse salt

Pear and Cranberry Relish

In a heavy saucepan, combine the pears, cranberries, sugar, vinegar, orange peel and juice, cayenne, and cinnamon. Bring the mixture to a boil. Reduce the heat, cover, and simmer for 15 minutes, stirring twice.

Transfer the relish to a serving bowl, cover, and chill for at least 4 hours, or as long as 4 days.

Just before serving, place the pecans in a skillet and toss over a medium heat until lightly browned. Fold the freshly toasted pecans into the relish.

YIELD: 6 CUPS.

4½ cups peeled, cored, and chopped pears (any variety, half ripe)
3½ cups cranberries
1½ cups sugar
½ cup apple cider vinegar
I tablespoon grated orange peel
½ cup fresh orange juice
⅛ teaspoon cayenne
I teaspoon ground cinnamon
I cup pecans

Crusty Oat Berry Bread

2½ cups whole oat berries
7½ cups warm water
3 tablespoons active dry yeast
1 cup molasses
4 cups rolled oats
1 tablespoon coarse salt
½ cup safflower oil
6 to 7 cups unbleached white flour

Bring 5 cups of the water to boil; pour over the oat berries and soak for at least 8 hours or overnight.

Butter three 9 x 5 x 3-inch loaf pans.

Combine remaining 2½ cups of the warm water, the yeast, molasses, and 3½ cups of the rolled oats in the bowl of an electric mixer. Stir to blend, and leave for 5 minutes, allowing the yeast to soften.

Add the oat berries, salt, safflower oil, and 3 cups of the flour. Mix at low speed for 5 minutes. Add another 2 cups of flour and mix 3 minutes more. Turn the dough out onto a flour-dusted countertop, and, using as much of the remaining flour as necessary, knead until smooth and elastic. Place the dough in a buttered bowl, turning it once. Cover with a kitchen towel and let rise in a warm place (a turned-off oven works well) for 1 hour, or until doubled in size.

Divide and shape the dough into 3 loaves, and place the loaves in the prepared pans. Sprinkle each top with some of the remaining rolled oats.

Let the loaves rise in a warm place for about 40 minutes, or until doubled in size.

Preheat the oven to 375 degrees.

Bake the loaves for 40 to 50 minutes, or until they sound hollow when lightly tapped. Remove from the pans and let cool on a wire rack. When completely cooled, place the loaves in plastic bags, and store at room temperature.

To serve, cut each loaf into 10 slices, or slice 1 loaf and place it with the other 2 loaves on a wooden board with a bread knife.

NOTE: Stored at room temperature in plastic bags, the loaves will keep for up to 4 days. Frozen, they will last up to 3 months.

YIELD: 3 LOAVES, 30 SLICES.

Linzer Schnitten

Preheat the oven to 350 degrees. Butter a 10 x 13 x 1-inch baking sheet.

Place 2½ cups of the flour in the bowl of an electric mixer. Add the sugar, hazelnuts, walnuts, cinnamon, cloves, and lemon peel. Mix well. Add the butter and 2 eggs. Mix at low speed until well blended, about 2 minutes.

Scrape the dough onto a flour-dusted countertop, and knead until smooth, about 30 seconds. Cut off one-quarter of the pastry and set aside.

Using your hands, pat the remaining dough into the prepared baking sheet. Spread the raspberry preserves over the pastry.

Roll the small piece of dough into a large rectangle about ⅛ inch thick. Using a sharp flour-dusted knife, cut the rectangle into ½-inch strips. Place the strips in a lattice pattern over the whole baking sheet, about 1¼ inches apart.

Beat the egg yolk with the heavy cream, and brush lightly over the lattice strips.

Bake 25 minutes, or until light brown. Cool.

When ready to serve, dust the torte with confectioners' sugar and cut the pastry into 2¼ x 1½-inch bars.

3 cups unbleached white flour
1¼ cups granulated sugar
1 cup finely ground hazelnuts
1 cup finely chopped walnuts
1 tablespoon ground cinnamon
¼ teaspoon ground cloves
1¼ teaspoons grated lemon peel
½ pound (2 sticks) cold butter, cut into 16 pieces
2 eggs
1⅓ cups raspberry preserves
1 egg yolk
1 tablespoon heavy cream
½ cup confectioners' sugar

YIELD: 56 BARS.

Orange-Currant Cake

This cake should rest for 24 hours before serving to allow the flavors to blend fully.

½ pound (2 sticks) butter, at room
    temperature
1¼ cups sugar
4 eggs
2 tablespoons grated orange peel
2 teaspoons grated lemon peel
2¼ cups unbleached white flour
1 teaspoon baking soda
¾ cup milk
1 cup currants

GLAZE

1 cup fresh orange juice
3 tablespoons lemon juice
½ cup sugar

Preheat the oven to 325 degrees.

Cream the butter and sugar until light. Add the eggs, one at a time, beating well after each addition. Add the grated orange and lemon peel. Mix the flour with the baking soda and add half of it to the batter. Add the milk, and beat until well blended. Add the remaining flour and the currants. Mix until all traces of flour are gone. The batter should be smooth.

Spoon the batter into a 9½-inch Kugelhopf pan, an 11-inch, 10-cup Bundt cake pan, or a tube pan with a 3-quart capacity. Smooth the top of the batter.

Bake 1 hour, or until a toothpick inserted in the center comes out clean.

Remove the cake from the oven, and let rest in the pan for 10 minutes.

To make the glaze, combine the orange juice, lemon juice, and sugar in a heavy saucepan. Stirring constantly over low heat, warm the mixture until the sugar melts. Spoon the warm juices over the cake. Let the cake absorb the juices for about 15 minutes. Unmold the cake onto a flat plate, and cool.

Wrapped in plastic, the cake can be stored in the refrigerator for at least 24 hours, or up to 8 days.

YIELD: 1 CAKE, APPROXIMATELY 32 THIN SLICES.

Sacher Torte

The original torte straight from the Sacher Hotel in Vienna is very rich, and should be served in very small portions. It is best made in stages, giving it time to absorb the liqueur and chocolate.

Preheat the oven to 250 degrees. Butter the bottom of a 9-inch springform pan.

Melt the chocolate in the preheated oven, then cool it to room temperature. Raise the oven temperature to 325 degrees.

Transfer the melted chocolate to a mixer bowl. Add the softened butter, and beat at high speed for 3 minutes. Add the 7 egg yolks and vanilla, and beat 3 minutes more. Fold in the flour.

In a clean bowl, beat the egg whites at high speed for 1 minute. With the mixer running, add the sugar in a steady stream, beating until thick and heavy, about 5 minutes.

Fold the beaten egg whites into the chocolate mixture. Pour the batter into the prepared pan. Bake 35 to 40 minutes, or until a toothpick inserted in the center comes out clean. Cool for at least 3 hours.

Loosen the sides of the pan, and slide the cake onto a flat plate. Sprinkle with Framboise.

In a small saucepan, combine the apricot preserves with the water, and heat to blend. Brush the top and sides of the cake with it, covering the cake completely. Let the preserves dry for at least 6 hours.

To finish the cake, melt the semisweet chocolate in a heavy saucepan over very low heat. Stirring constantly, add ⅓ cup cream. Remove from the heat and stir in the butter. If the glaze separates, add 1 more tablespoon of heavy cream.

Pour the glaze over the cake, tilting it slowly so the glaze runs down the sides. Let set for 1 hour.

NOTE: This cake will keep for 3 days at room temperature.

½ pound unsweetened imported chocolate

½ pound (2 sticks) butter, at room temperature

7 eggs, separated, at room temperature

2 teaspoons vanilla extract

¾ cup unbleached white flour

1¼ cups sugar

FIRST GLAZE

¼ cup Framboise liqueur

⅔ cup apricot preserves

1 tablespoon water

SECOND GLAZE

3 ounces semisweet Belgian chocolate

Heavy cream

2 tablespoons cold butter

YIELD: 30 SMALL PIECES.

APRÈS SKATING SUPPER
FOR TWELVE

HOT SPICED WINE

ARUGULA AND AVOCADO SALAD

SESAME BREAD STICKS

LAMB, ONION, AND BUTTERNUT SQUASH STEW

BUTTERED ANGEL HAIR PASTA

BRUSSELS SPROUTS SAUTÉ

ORANGES WITH CHAMPAGNE SABAYON

CHOCOLATE CLUSTERS

There is a beautiful beaver pond, about a mile or so down the road from Loaves and Fishes, that in the winter becomes a favorite spot for ice skating. Recently, Detlef and I gave a party for our entire family and some friends that was more than just a meal. We gathered at the pond in the late afternoon, bundled up against the chill, and for a couple of hours we glided around, trying to stay upright while our noses turned pink with cold. It was great fun. Before the sun set we returned home, where I presented everyone with a steaming mug of Hot Spiced Wine that had been heated on the stove. Everyone gathered near the fireplace to warm up. The stew was in the oven, the desserts were on the counter, the salad and vegetables only needed finishing touches—that's the beauty of this menu. Almost all of it can be prepared well in advance.

The salad can be assembled that morning, and everything except the avocados can be stored in a plastic bag or damp towel in the refrigerator. At the very last minute, peel and quarter the avocados, add them to the salad, and toss lightly with dressing.

The stew can be made up to 4 days ahead. Cover and store it in the refrigerator, and on the day of the party, bring it to room temperature before baking in a preheated 350-degree oven for 45 minutes.

The Brussels sprouts can be sliced the day before, stored in a covered container in the refrigerator, and sautéed just before serving.

Both desserts can be made up to 2 days in advance. The Oranges with Champagne Sabayon should be covered and stored in the refrigerator, and the Chocolate Clusters should be placed in an airtight container and left at room temperature. This leaves you only the pasta to whip together at the last minute.

This menu need not be restricted to a skating party—it's fabulous for any gathering on a snowy winter night.

Hot Spiced Wine

Except for 12 of the cinnamon sticks, combine all the ingredients in a heavy stainless-steel saucepan. Heat until hot, but not boiling. Remove the solids, and pour into glass or ceramic mugs. Add a cinnamon stick to each mug for stirring, and serve hot.

3 bottles red wine (preferably Burgundy)
3 cloves
15 cinnamon sticks
Peel of 1 orange (left whole)
½ cup sugar

YIELD: 12 SERVINGS.

Arugula and Avocado Salad

Form an outer circle of arugula leaves on 12 salad plates. Using 2 mushrooms for each plate, arrange the slices in a circle on the inside of the leaves, leaving enough room in the center for an avocado quarter. Sprinkle the minced red onion over each salad.

Combine the dressing ingredients in a screw-top jar. Shake vigorously. Spoon the dressing over each salad. Serve with sesame bread sticks, or any crusty French bread.

4 bunches arugula or watercress, washed and dried
24 white mushrooms, thinly sliced
3 ripe avocados, peeled and cut into quarters
1 cup minced red onions

DRESSING

1 cup extra-virgin olive oil
¼ cup Balsamic vinegar
¼ teaspoon Tabasco
2 teaspoons coarse salt
24 fresh crisp sesame bread sticks, or
1 loaf crusty French bread

YIELD: 12 SERVINGS.

Lamb, Onion, and Butternut Squash Stew

⅓ cup olive oil

Two 7 to 8-pound legs of lamb, boned,
   trimmed of all fat, and cut into
   1½-inch chunks (about 6½ pounds
   meat)

4 cups coarsely chopped onions

1 tablespoon minced garlic

3 cups coarsely chopped butternut
   squash

2 tablespoons seeded and minced
   jalapeño pepper

3 tablespoons unbleached white flour

1 tablespoon coarse salt

1 teaspoon freshly ground black pepper

1 tablespoon ground coriander

1 tablespoon ground cumin

1½ teaspoons ground cinnamon

1½ cups red wine, preferably
   Burgundy

2 cups chicken stock (page 8)

3 cups coarsely chopped canned plum
   tomatoes with their juices

½ cup finely chopped fresh parsley

Preheat the oven to 350 degrees.

Heat the olive oil in a large heavy sauté pan. Brown the lamb in the oil over medium-high heat for about 10 minutes. Add the onions, and sauté 5 minutes, stirring a few times. Stir in the next 9 ingredients, blending well. Add the wine, stock, and tomatoes. Stir well, and bring to a boil. Cover the pan, and place in the oven. Bake for 2 hours.

To serve, place the stew in a large tureen or serving bowl. Garnish with parsley.

YIELD: 12 SERVINGS.

Buttered Angel Hair Pasta

Fill a 5-quart pot three-quarters full of salted water. Bring to a rolling boil, add the pasta, and watch carefully. Fresh pasta will be done in the time it takes for the water to return to a boil, about 2 minutes. Remove a strand with a fork, and test to make sure it is al dente. Drain the pasta in a large colander, place in a bowl, add the butter, garlic, and parsley, toss well, and serve.

2½ pounds fresh angel hair pasta
6 tablespoons butter
2 teaspoons minced garlic
¼ cup chopped fresh parsley

YIELD: 12 SERVINGS.

Brussels Sprouts Sauté

Rinse and dry the Brussels sprouts. Cut off and discard the hard ends, and thinly slice the sprouts.

Heat the butter in a large sauté pan. Add the sliced Brussels sprouts, cover, and sauté over low heat for about 8 minutes. When done, the sprouts should be crisp and deep green. Sprinkle with salt and pepper, and serve with the stew.

3 pounds fresh Brussels sprouts
½ cup clarified butter
1½ teaspoons coarse salt
1½ teaspoons freshly ground black pepper

YIELD: 12 SERVINGS.

Oranges with Champagne Sabayon

A variation of zabaglione, this deluxe sauce is wonderful with fresh berries in season, sliced peaches, or over any pound cake.

ORANGES

8 navel oranges

2 cups sugar

3 cups water

Peel of 2 oranges, cut into thin strips

CHAMPAGNE SABAYON

8 egg yolks

I cup sugar

2 cups dry champagne

¼ cup Grand Marnier

Peel and cut each orange in half lengthwise. Slice into ¼-inch half-moon slices. Place in a glass bowl.

In a small saucepan, combine the sugar, water, and orange peel, and bring to a boil. Reduce the heat, and simmer for 10 minutes. Pour the syrup over the oranges, and chill.

To make the sabayon, place the egg yolks and sugar in a medium-size mixing bowl placed over a saucepan of simmering water. Beat the eggs with a wire whisk for about 3 minutes, until foamy. Add the champagne, and continue whisking until the mixture starts to thicken, about 10 minutes. Remove from the heat and add the Grand Marnier. Stir gently before serving. To serve, divide the sabayon among 12 dessert glasses. Spoon the oranges into the sabayon, dropping them into the center of each glass.

The sabayon can be served either warm or chilled.

YIELD: 12 SERVINGS.

Chocolate Clusters

To enjoy these luscious treats at their best, keep them at room temperature.

Place the chocolate pieces and the corn syrup in the top of a double boiler, over simmering hot water. Stir until melted. Add the raisins.

Drop the chocolate mixture 1 teaspoon at a time on a sheet of parchment or wax paper. Allow the clusters to firm up at room temperature. Serve.

6 ounces semisweet chocolate, broken into small pieces
1 tablespoon light corn syrup
1 cup firmly packed dark raisins

YIELD: 3 DOZEN CLUSTERS.

INDEX